ALTERNATIVE CHICAGO

ALTERNATIVE CHICAGO

Unique Destinations Beyond the Magnificent Mile

SECOND EDITION

BILL FRANZ

Cumberland House
Nashville, Tennessee

Copyright © 2000, 2004 by Bill Franz

Published by
Cumberland House Publishing, Inc.
431 Harding Industrial Drive
Nashville, TN 37211

Cover design: James Duncan
Interior design: Mary Sanford

Library of Congress Cataloging-in-Publication Data
Franz, Bill (William), 1967-
  Alternative Chicago : unique destinations beyond the Magnificent Mile
/ Bill Franz.— 2nd ed.
     p. cm.
  Includes index.
  ISBN 978-1-68162-625-4
  1. Chicago (Ill.)—Guidebooks. I. Title.
  F548.18.F73 2004
  917.73'1104—dc22

                                                    2003027513

Printed in the United States of America
1 2 3 4 5 6 —09 08 07 06 05 04

*To my wife, Yanti, who puts up with
my many addlepated schemes and notions,
and to the two-legged little mongrel as well.*

A Guide to the Symbols in This Book

 Bar/Club

 Books/Magazines/Comics/
'Zines/Posters

 Clothing

 Coffee

 Food

 Furniture/Knickknacks

 Head Shop/Tattoo
Parlor/Hippie Hangout

 Liquor Store

 Live Music/Theater/
Performance

XXX Pornography/Sex Shop

 Records/Tapes/CDs/Music

 Shoes

 Videos/DVDs
(Rental/Purchase)

Contents

Introduction

Unlike many guidebooks, this one is not going to tell you where to stay or how to get around the city, or even what particular sights you should see. There are already dozens of guidebooks that concentrate on those very subjects—one of which you probably already have. This guidebook won't tell you which fancy, expensive restaurants to frequent or which ritzy boutiques to visit. Instead you'll get a neighborhood-by-neighborhood account of the places *you* want to know about—resale and vintage shops, record stores and bookstores, offbeat eateries and cool bars and clubs. Those regular guidebooks are impersonal at best; at worst they assume their readers are carrying around enough cash to finance a small, third-world nation. Think of them as guidebooks for your parents. This is *not* your parents' guidebook. This guidebook is for younger, more discriminating folk. And by younger, I don't just mean chronologically, but young at heart. You can be sixteen or sixty and still appreciate this book. You don't have to be under thirty to appreciate unique, independently owned establishments, which are primarily what is covered here, along with local and regional chains. You won't find out where the nearest Borders Books or Tower Records is located, but you will find local institutions like Bookworks and Hi-Fi

Records. No Hard Rock Cafe or Planet Hollywood, but how about Clubfoot Lounge and Heartland Cafe? Never heard of these joints? Of course you haven't. Nor have you heard of Land of the Lost Vintage or Una Mae's Freak Boutique. These are all distinctly Chicago places, and that's what you'll find out about here—neighborhood by neighborhood.

ORGANIZATION

After quite a bit of inner debate, I decided the most organized way to present these various neighborhoods was to begin in that section of the city most visible to newcomers—the Loop. This is where all the skyscrapers and businesspeople cluster. Though you'll probably spend most of your time north of here, it's a convenient starting point. From the Loop we will proceed directly north, sweeping outward and up. It is, after all, the North Side where you'll find most of Chicago's premier shopping, eating, and carousing joints. (That said, we will deviate slightly from this pattern right off the bat. After the Loop, I'll discuss the South Loop, as you can explore both within the same day. For the remainder of the book, however, the pattern will hold steady.) After the North Side is finished, we'll start in Greek Town and sweep downward. Though geographically larger than the North Side, the South Side—with the exception of Hyde Park—is primarily residential and "unhip." Whereas many North Side residents are transplanted suburbanites and Midwesterners, south siders were generally born in the same neighborhoods in which they reside. Though the shopping opportunities are much more limited here than up north, you'll find that the South Side is very much worth the pilgrimage for its food. There are some excellent joints down here, as well as a few Chicago delicacies such as the Italian breaded-steak sandwich, that you won't want to miss.

CHICAGO—A VERY BRIEF HISTORY

Back in the 1600s, the present-day site of Chicago didn't have much to recommend it as a place of habitation. Even the local Potawatomi Indians avoided the windswept marsh on the shores of Lake Michigan. In 1673, however, French explorer Louis Joliet and Jesuit priest Jacques Marquette made their way through the region, which the Indians called *Checagou*, meaning "the place of the wild onion." Joliet immediately recognized the importance of the area. Ships could find a sheltered harbor in Lake Michigan, and from there trading boats could traverse the Chicago, Des Plaines, and Illinois Rivers to the Mississippi and New Orleans. Of course that was assuming that the canal Joliet envisioned between the Chicago and Des Plaines Rivers was built. Until then the muddy, five-mile portage boaters had to endure would continue to be a major impediment to the free flow of goods and people.

Joliet's canal was an idea that would lay dormant for many years, and over a hundred years would pass before the region acquired its first non-Indian inhabitant. This was in 1779, when Jean Baptiste du Sable—who was of mixed white/African ancestry—established a trading post. A handful of other traders began arriving over the next couple of decades, and in 1803 the U.S. government established Fort Dearborn at the site of what is now the intersection of Michigan Avenue and Wacker Drive on the outer edges of the Loop. The fort was established not only to protect the harbor and inland waterway, but to siphon the Indian trade away from the British, who were still allowed to operate in what is now Wisconsin. Chicago gained its first bit of notoriety during the War of 1812, when the entire garrison of the fort and the village's inhabitants were either killed or captured by an overwhelming force of Indians. Due to U.S. reversals in the war, the military commander had been ordered to abandon the fort and march the garrison to Indiana. Less than two miles from the fort the group was ambushed by Indians—Potawatomis, for the most part—among the sand dunes along Lake Michigan. That was the extent of Indian-white violence in Chicago, though the so-called "Winnebago War" of 1827 ("Winnebago Scare" would have been more fitting) and the much more appropriately named Black Hawk War of 1832 would send Chicago's residents into a panic. And rightly so—had the Potawatomis decided en masse to join forces with the "hostiles" of those two conflicts, they could have wiped Chicago off the map.

This led to the Chicago Treaty of 1833—the most expensive Indian treaty of its time. By its tenets, the Potawatomis agreed to completely relinquish all lands east of the Mississippi and to move west of the river. White settlement had been increasing throughout northern Illinois and southern Wisconsin for some time, and Chicago itself was beginning to boom now that plans were finally afoot to build Joilet's canal. This, combined with the massive military response to Black Hawk, had convinced the Potawatomis their time in the region was at an end. They could either take the money being offered and leave peacefully or face annihilation. Interestingly enough, for a tribe that had long adopted many white ways of dress and lifestyle, they decided to leave the city with a last display of "Indianness." Some eight hundred warriors, naked and painted, war-danced their way out of the city, much to the fascination of white onlookers—a number of whom were freshly arrived from the east and had never seen a "wild injun." The Potawatomis, apparently, got the effect they were hoping for. As one observer later commented, "The question forced itself on even those who had seen them most, what if they should, in their maddened frenzy, turn this sham warfare into a real attack? How easy it would be for them to massacre us all, and leave not a living soul to tell the story."

From here it was only a handful of decades before Chicago went from being a mud-choked, frontier outpost to one of the world's leading grain, lumber, railroad, and meat-packing centers, gathering the riches of the west before sending them on to New York and the rest of the world. Indeed, even the modern futures market as we know it today had its origins here, developing out of the grain trade.

But if Chicago was something before the Great Fire of 1871, when almost the entire city was razed, it was really amazing what happened afterward. Within twenty years it was rebuilt bigger than before, becoming the world's first skyscraper city.

Amid all the construction and industry, however, there were undercurrents of unrest. Workers often labored under appalling conditions and long hours, many of them living in overcrowded slums crawling with rats and disease. Though the influx of thousands of German and Bohemian immigrants had given rise to an active labor movement and socialist party, wealthy industrialists didn't exactly feel the need to listen to grievances considering they had a ready supply of cheap, immigrant labor to exploit. Chicago elections weren't exactly on the up-and-up, either. Vote fraud, ballot-stuffing, and intimidating gangs of thugs loitering about the polling places were the order of the day. Socialists soon grew disenchanted with their hopes of success through politics and began advocating revolution. Anarchist organizations began forming—their demonstrations and declarations in various newsletters greatly troubling the wealthy. Tensions continued to mount on both sides.

Things came to a head in 1886, as hundreds of strikes in support of an eight-hour workday took place across the country. A nationwide general strike was called for on May 1, and tens of thousands of Chicago workers participated. On May 4, a rally was held in Haymarket Square. This was a non-violent affair, as even Mayor Carter Harrison—who had attended the rally—would later testify. The mayor had left by the time the meeting was breaking up, and this was when the police chief sent in the troops. As riot police—pistols in hand—marched toward a clump of stragglers listening to the tail end of a speech, a bomb was thrown into their midst, scattering the cops in all directions. In the ensuing chaos, the police opened fire, as did those workers who were also armed. Seven cops died and sixty were wounded. There was never an official count of the casualties among the workers, but it is presumed they were about the same as those suffered by the police.

This incident was tragic enough, but the authorities soon made a travesty of it. Eight anarchist leaders were arrested for the incident and subjected to a farce of a trial, and seven of them were sentenced to hang, even though only two of them had actually been present at the scene. As the prosecutor himself declared: "These men are no more guilty than the thousands who follow them. Gentlemen of the jury, convict these men, make an example of them, hang them and save our institutions, our society." Three had their sentences commuted to life in prison and one committed suicide in his cell, but the other four—due to the refusal of department-store magnate Marshall Field to go along with the wishes of his peers and grant them clemency—were hanged less than a year later. In 1893, John Peter Altgeld, the governor of Illinois, pardoned the three still in prison, harshly denouncing the trial that had condemned them and the judge who had presided over it.

Not surprisingly, this incident did not cast the movers and shakers of the city into deep bouts of self-recrimination. Far from it. Business continued booming and strikers were easily replaced or beaten into submission as thousands upon thousands of destitute immigrants continued to pour into the city. More skyscrapers appeared, and Chicago's downtown became a marvel to behold. This earned the city the distinction of hosting the World's Columbian Exposition of 1893—a decidedly non–politically correct celebration of the four hundred years of civilization Columbus had unleashed upon the Americas.

As the century turned, Chicago continued to grow, its factories and stockyards among the world's busiest. World War I brought the first large influx of black emigrants to the city. Since thousands of white workers had joined the army, southern blacks moved north to fill the vacancies, as well as to escape the oppression of the south. Chicago, however, was no bastion of racial egalitarianism. On one particularly hot summer day in 1919, a black boy drowned after being knocked unconscious by a rock when his makeshift raft floated into the "white section" of Lake Michigan. The incident spawned a violent race riot in which fifteen whites and twenty-three blacks were killed.

Prohibition became the law of the land the following January, and before long Al Capone was running the underworld, adding another memorable spate of violence to the city's rich history with the St. Valentine's Day Massacre of 1929. Capone was out of the picture by the early '30s, but by then the Great Depression was hanging heavy over the city and nation. Things didn't much improve until the hyperproduction of World War II. In 1942 Chicago was the site of another somewhat infamous event. Enrico Fermi and his cohorts at the University of Chicago managed to achieve the world's first self-sustaining nuclear reaction. The residents of Hiroshima and Nagasaki are still applauding that one.

The year 1955 ushered in the arrival of "Da Mare": Richard J. Daley. He would rule the city with an iron fist, as many across the country realized during the '68 Democratic Convention. This event was a gleeful period for Chicago police, who had Daley's blessing to club and beat hippie demonstrators to their hearts' content—not to mention a number of reporters, a priest or two, and many an average

Joe and Jane who simply stumbled into the chaos on their way home from work.

Daley died in 1976, and before his son, Richard M., could permanently replace him in '89, Chicago had its first female mayor, Jane Byrne, and its first African American mayor, Harold Washington. Ol' Richey M. is firmly in place now, and will run the city until he either appoints a successor or drops dead in office like his father. Challengers are so few and far between that four years back Daley would have run completely unopposed if it hadn't been for the last-minute, sacrificial candidacy of Illinois Congressman and fellow Democrat (and former Black Panther) Bobby Rush. Republicans, for their part, have simply written Chicago off and don't even bother to challenge Daley.

After a period of stagnation through the '70s and early '80s, Chicago entered a boom period in the mid-'90s. From manufacturing to banking to coffee-slinging, jobs were plentiful, large sections of the city were gentrified, and new construction was everywhere, especially in neighborhoods close to downtown. Though this has eased up a bit, jobs are still available, and plenty of money is still being made in real estate and construction, leading to a sharp rise in the price of housing from the affordable rates of only some five years ago. Chicago, like many other top-tier cities, is becoming an increasingly expensive place to live, as traditionally working-class neighborhoods become the sole domain of professionals.

On a lighter note, another big change from the mid-'90s is the transformation of the Michael Jordan–era Bulls from perennial champs to the butt of the NBA. Outside of one wild season in '01 by the Bears, no other Chicago sports team had excited anything close to the same level of interest until the Cubs made their run at the World Series in 2003. Having not regularly followed baseball for years, I thoroughly believed the hype being pushed in the *Chicago Tribune* that the Cubs would easily win the series. (Could this have been because the *Trib* actually owns the Cubs? Nah. . . .) It wasn't until about the sixth inning of the last game of the National League title match that I suddenly had the abrupt realization that the Cubs might blow it. Historians of the Cubs should have suspected much sooner, though some chose to blame an overzealous fan's catch of a foul ball and/or an ancient curse involving a pet goat rather than the team itself. Though statistically the Cubs won't have another shot at the Series until about 2063, you'll still find that Chicagoans have plenty to boast about—you know, like the levels of corruption and Daley-worship in which their aldermanic officials indulge, not to mention the girth of their policemen. It may sound corny, but Chicago is a city that is quite simply adored by most of its residents. It may be true that Chicago is the "Second City" (or, more properly nowadays, the Third), but most Chicagoans will tell you that that designation is purely a technicality.

ALTERNATIVE CHICAGO

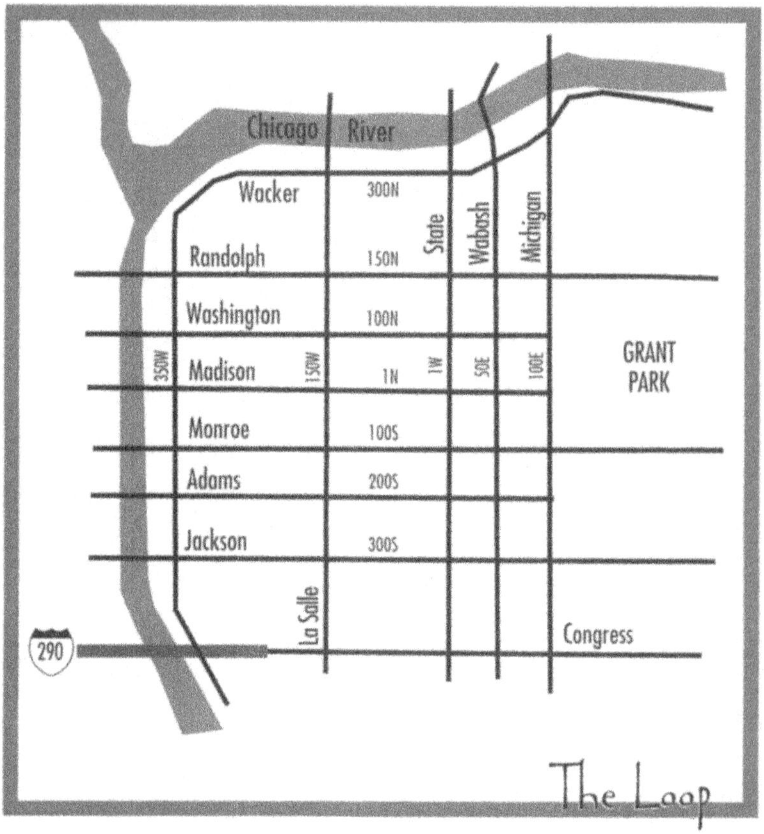
Chicago River
Wacker
300N
Randolph
150N
State
Wabash
Michigan
Washington
100N
350W
Madison
150W
1N
1W
50E
100E
GRANT PARK
Monroe
100S
Adams
200S
Jackson
300S
La Salle
290
Congress
The Loop

THE LOOP

This is where Chicago sprang into the city it is now, growing up around a spot near the Chicago River called Wolf Point, near the massive Merchandise Mart at Wacker Drive and Lake Street. Today you can descend a flight of steps down to the riverbank and eat your lunch overlooking the spot where Mark Beaubien, an early tavern keeper, used to sit on his porch picking off ducks with his shotgun over 170 years ago.

From what was a hodgepodge assemblage of a few taverns in 1830 frequented by French trappers, Indians, and half-bloods, a real live city grew into being only ten short years later. Back then the Loop was the city limits, and all business was conducted in its confines; the adjacent neighborhoods were suburbs or small villages. By 1870 the Loop was known for its huge buildings, the appalling clouds of black smoke and soot hovering overhead, the crush of its wagon and railroad traffic, and its overcrowded mass of humanity. But then came the Great Fire of 1871, leveling the entire area. By 1890 it was completely rebuilt on a more massive scale then before, with several of the world's first skyscrapers making an appearance. The growth continued up until the eve of the Great Depression, and then it wasn't until the 1980s that it really picked back up again. The Loop now sports dozens of new skyscrapers, and more were under construction as late as the '90s.

The Loop—named after the loop of the elevated subway tracks—is where the city's banking and financial business is done, as well as most government activities. During rush hours and lunch times, nattily attired business folk—from receptionists to CEOs—dart about everywhere, filling the scores of eateries and coffee shops. You'll find a wide array of businesses here, most of them catering to big spenders. As far as food is concerned, though, you can get anything from a gourmet meal to a cheap hot dog.

Within the Loop's confines are Grant Park along the Lake, the Art Institute on Michigan Avenue, and Buckingham Fountain, along with several historical buildings like the Auditorium Theater, the Monadnock Building, and, of course, the Sears Tower. The Loop is very congested and parking is practically an impossibility, but you shouldn't leave Chicago without spending at least a few hours strolling about its streets.

Rain Dog Books

404 S. Michigan Avenue 312-922-1200
Hours: Mon-Sat, 11 A.M.–6 P.M.; Sun, 12 P.M.–5 P.M.

If you'd like to step back for a while into the "genteel world" of the old-school bookstore, this is your place. Rain Dog specializes in antiquarian books. Everything here is old, rare, and expensive.

The Savvy Traveler

310 S. Michigan Avenue 312-913-9800
Hours: Mon-Sat, 10 A.M.–7:30 P.M.; Sun, 12 P.M.–5 P.M.

Here you'll find an outstanding collection of travel books and maps for every region of the world, catering to every type of traveler, as well as videos, DVDs, and a few CDs. They also sell travel accessories and luggage, along with a great collection of coffee-table photo books. Chicago's premier place to hit if you're planning a trip to somewhere a bit out there. Now you can finally find a guidebook for that trip to Inner Mongolia you've been planning.

Chicago Architecture Foundation

224 S. Michigan Avenue 312-922-3432
Hours: Mon–Sat, 9 A.M.–6:30 P.M., Sun, 9:30 A.M.–6 P.M.

For those with an interest in architecture, this is a place designed to make you spend a whole lot of cash. They stock great picture books and videos, along with stained glass panels, lamps, models, toys, and various knickknacks—not to mention a stunning array of decorative cow figurines.

Prairie Avenue Bookshop

418 S. Wabash Avenue 312-922-8311
Hours: Mon–Fri, 10 A.M.–6 P.M., Sat, 10 A.M.–4 P.M.

Another place for the architecture aficionado. This store is dedicated solely to that medium. Here you'll find plenty of picture books and biographies, but also numerous books on theory as well as the technical and administrative side of the business. They also have a section upstairs devoted to rare and out-of-print works, where you'll find several old Chicago city documents and plans.

Exchequer Pub

226 S. Wabash Avenue 312-939-5633
Hours: Mon–Thu, 11 A.M.–11 P.M.; Fri–Sat, 11 A.M.–
12 A.M.; Sun, 12 P.M.–9 P.M.

If you're looking for a decent place to drink and eat in the Loop, I'd suggest the Exchequer Pub. It fills up with businesspeople and can get quite loud, but it's a nice, dim, old-style pub. They also serve up a damn good bowl of French onion soup.

Ragstock

226 S. Wabash Avenue, 2nd Floor 312-692-1778
Hours: Mon-Fri, 10 A.M.–8 P.M.; Sat, 10 A.M.–7 P.M.; Sun,
12 P.M.–6 P.M.

This Midwestern chain based in Minnesota boasts two stores in the city. Here you'll find a good selection of new and used clothing at decent prices as well as sunglasses, cheap wigs, and various other accessories. The merchandise tends towards the more outlandish and retro, but there are plenty of basic t-shirts and hoodies and such to cater to almost every taste. This is a pleasant, laid-back place that won't take a big chunk out of your wallet.

North Loop Comics

226 S. Wabash Avenue, 6th Floor 312-922-6585
Hours: Mon-Sat, 11 A.M.–5:30 P.M.

After a journey made possible by a real-life elevator operator, you'll arrive in a quiet hall. Follow its snaking pattern and voilà—you've reached North Loop Comics. This little cubbyhole of a shop is not very browser-friendly, as the owner conducts most of his business through mail-order. A number of new comics are on display, with several more in boxes scattered about the place. I would suggest calling first before stopping by. If you do just drop in, it would be a good idea to know exactly what you're looking for, for the proprietor is one of the most ineffective salesmen you're likely to come across. Loquacious he is not. All the same, this place is definitely worth checking out if you're a collector.

Afrocentric Bookstore

333 S. State Street (Music Mart) 312-939-1956
Hours: Mon–Fri, 9:30 A.M.–6:30 P.M.; Sat, 10 A.M.–5 P.M.

This small, sunny, attractive shop sells new books along with incense and greeting cards. The topics, of course, deal with African American themes, and range from fiction to Christianity. The history section is particularly good, and they also have a great selection of conspiracy books.

Crow's Nest Music

333 S. State Street (Music Mart) 312-341-9196
Hours: Mon–Fri, 9 A.M.–8 P.M., Sat, 9 A.M.–7 P.M.,
Sun, 11 A.M.–5 P.M.

Though a huge, slick store that looks very corporate and "Blockbuster"-like, this place actually specializes in imports and rarities. You'll be surprised at the amount of quality stuff they have. All forms of music are extensively represented, with amazing back catalogs of even obscure groups like Negativland. Their DVD collection is also outstanding. Though possibly a bit more expensive than you'd like, this place is well worth checking out for the hard-to-find stuff.

Books-a-Million

144 S. Clark Street 312-857-0613
Hours: Mon–Fri, 7:30 A.M.–6 P.M.; Sat, 10 A.M.–5 P.M.

This store carries an unremarkable collection of new books and magazines. If you're looking for the latest mass-market paperback novel, you'll be sure to find it here, though they do carry a number of classics and trade paperbacks as well. All in all, they have a decent, general selection of stuff. In fact—if you'll allow me to indulge in simile—this place is like a fast-food joint in that they have plenty of fare to appeal to your immediate hunger, but nothing that will satisfy you as much as a real meal.

Graham Crackers Comics

69 E. Madison Avenue 312-629-1810
Hours: Mon–Tue, 10 A.M.–6 P.M.; Wed, 10 A.M.–6:30 P.M.;
Thu–Fri, 10 A.M.–6 P.M.; Sat, 11 A.M.–5 P.M.; Sun,
12 P.M.–5 P.M.

One of two Graham Crackers stores in Chicago, this shop stocks a large selection of new comics and graphic novels—both mainstream and small press.

Their collection of back issues on the second floor is fairly extensive, and they also sell a smattering of models, toys, and posters.

Rock Records

175 W. Washington Street 312-346-3489
Hours: Mon–Fri, 9 A.M.–6:30 P.M.; Sat, 10 A.M.–4 P.M.

 This expansive store offers a solid, general selection of new CDs and DVDs. They do carry a number of independent-label artists, but you're not going to find anything too obscure here. Prices, especially on back-catalog stuff, are quite reasonable.

Brent's Books and Cards

309 W. Washington Street 312-364-0126
Hours: Mon–Fri, 8 A.M.–7 P.M.

Just as Rock Records offers a solid, general selection of music, so does Brent's offer a solid, general selection of new books. You can find the bestsellers here, along with plenty of other works, but nothing too out there. They also carry greeting cards and plenty of magazines.

2

SOUTH LOOP

The South Loop is much more sedate than the Loop proper. Many condos are popping up in place of the transient hotels that used to be peppered liberally throughout the area. Consequently some nightlife has begun to appear, but for the most part you'll find the South Loop relatively quiet, with a number of low-key businesses spread throughout. Roosevelt University and my own alma mater—Columbia College—are in the South Loop, as well as the Sperticus Museum of Judaica, the Shedd Aquarium, the Field Museum, and the Adler Planetarium.

Sandmeyer's Bookstore

714 S. Dearborn Street 312-922-2104
Hours: Tue–Fri, 11 A.M.–6:30 P.M.;
Sat, 11 A.M.–5 P.M.; Sun, 12 P.M.–5 P.M.

This is a sleekly designed, sunny store with a decent general selection of new books. No particular section is all that large, but what they do stock is all quality stuff—no Tom Clancy or Danielle Steele here. They also sell postcards and "artsy" greeting cards.

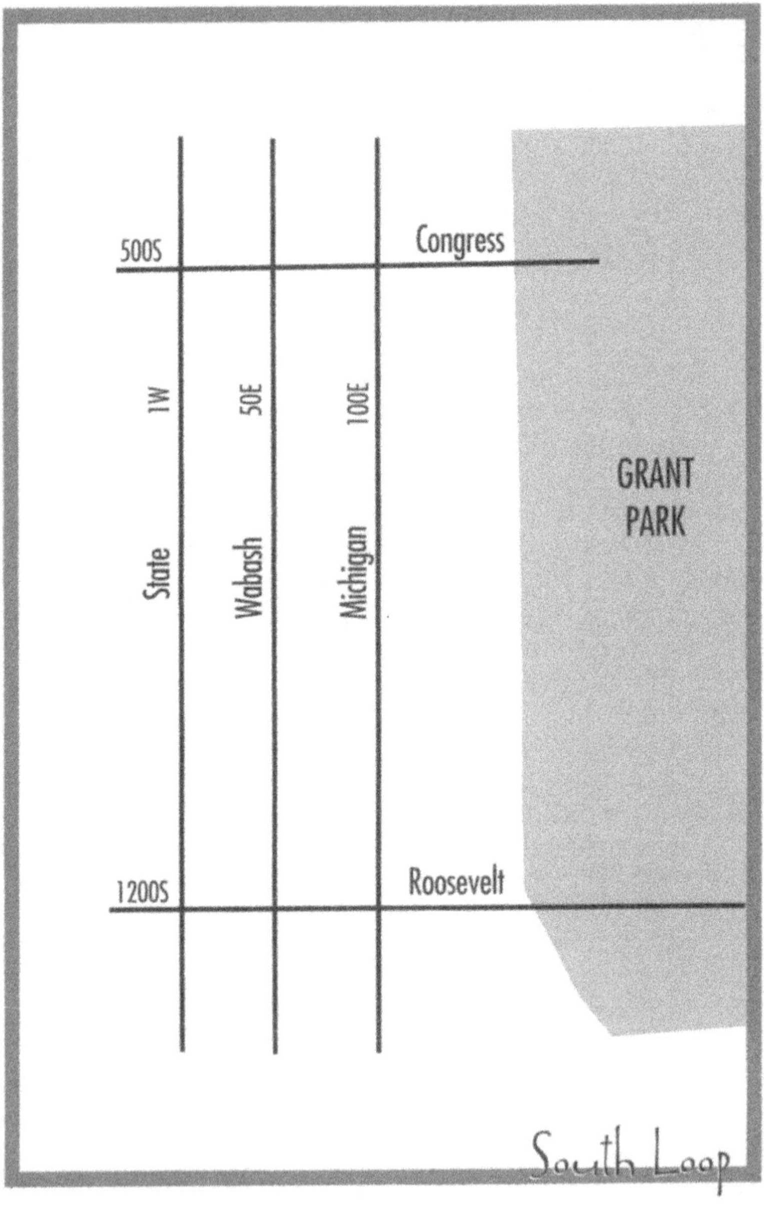
500S
Congress
1W
State
50E
Wabash
100E
Michigan
GRANT PARK
1200S
Roosevelt
South Loop

Printer's Row Fine and Rare Books

715 S. Dearborn Street 312-583-1800
Hours: Tue–Fri, 10 A.M.–7 P.M.; Sat–Sun, 11 A.M.–5 P.M.

This "old-school" bookstore has a small but excellent collection of first editions and collected-works sets. Most of the titles are early to mid-twentieth century novels, but you will find some nineteenth-century works here too. Essentially, this place is designed for book collectors, rather than someone looking for obscure works such as early nineteenth-century travel narratives dealing with Illinois and Wisconsin that shed light on Indian-white relations during the period, which—I admit—I've been keeping my eye out for of late. But if I was in the market for a first edition copy of Jack Kerouac's *Dharma Bums* or any number of works by other renowned writers, this would be my place of choice.

Buddy Guy's Legends

754 S. Wabash Avenue 312-427-0333
Hours: Mon–Thu, 5 P.M.–2 A.M.; Fri, 4 P.M.–2 A.M.;

Sat, 5 P.M.–3 A.M.; Sun, 6 P.M.–2 A.M.

One of Chicago's best blues clubs, this place is indeed part-owned by Chicago legend Buddy Guy. Live music is featured every night, and many of the acts passing through are nationally known. They also serve up cajun food until midnight. This is some good, classic stuff: jambalaya, red beans and rice, and fried catfish. They also serve po' boys, but I must say I'm a bit leery of their authenticity since they're served open-faced.

Hot House

31 E. Balbo Drive 312-362-9707
Hours: Varies; call ahead for showtimes

Originally located in Wicker Park, Hot House went on hiatus for a while before acquiring these new digs. They definitely have a nice space here, but, of course, they're facing licensing trouble from the city, so it might not last. That would be a shame, for Hot House is the place to go for world music. African and Latin American musicians play here regularly, and they also host plenty of jazz bands in between. In addition they stage plays, film screenings, and readings—not to mention various workshops. Think of Hot House as your all-purpose arts complex.

Powell's Bookstore

 828 S. Wabash Avenue 312-341-0748
Hours: Mon–Fri, 10:30 A.M.–6 P.M.; Sat, 10 A.M.–6 P.M.;
Sun, 12 P.M.–5 P.M.

Though larger, this Powell's is not too different from the others in the city. Upstairs you'll find the big-ticket art books and newer fiction and such. Downstairs, hell, it's a virtual warehouse. Row after row of books spread out around you, along with discount tables. You could literally spend an entire day here and still only scratch the surface.

3

WEST LOOP

Over the past decade this industrial, commercial area has obtained a residential flavor, with scores of expensive new condos and lofts sprouting up amid the existing businesses. This neighborhood is part of the famous Near West Side, which served as a congested habitat for thousands of immigrants in the late nineteenth century, though the worst slums were further south and west. The area is still best known for the Fulton Street Market, where chefs and restauranteurs purchase their meats and produce. In fact, many a yuppie who moved into the neighborhood soon complained about all the trucks and early-morning bustle. Asked to respond to the issue, Mayor Daley—wisely in this case—had little compassion. "Hey, whattaya gonna do," he simply shrugged, "it's a marketplace." The residential nature of the place is hard to ignore these days, however. I used to work in the area some years back, and I must say the sleek façades of the new condos that have materialized everywhere can be somewhat disorienting to someone who remembers the rather forlorn, gritty atmosphere of a decade ago. Back then, it wasn't unusual to see an occasional prostitute on Madison Avenue at six in

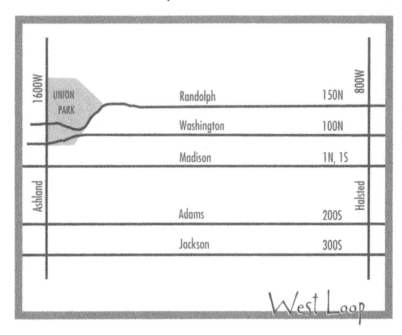

the morning on your way to work—sometimes even dazed, battered-looking ones walking down the middle of the street in the dead of winter with exposed breasts. Compared to those days of yore, kiddies, I'd have to conclude that gentrification is not always such a bad thing. What you'll find here now, for the most part, are a handful of pricey restaurants and a shifting cast of trendy clubs, most of them on Randolph and Madison, the main drags.

Hi Ricky Asia Noodle Shop
941 W. Randolph Street 312-491-9100
Hours: Sun–Thu, 11 A.M.–10 P.M.; Fri–Sat, 12 P.M.–11 P.M.

This is one of several Hi Ricky restaurants throughout Chicagoland (yes, Chicago metropolitan residents do use that term with a straight face). The menu is distinctly pan-Asian, or—I would say if didn't sound so clumsy—pan–Southeast Asian. Fried and soupy noodle dishes from Thailand to Indonesia and every country in between are the highlight of the menu, though they also have plenty of rice dishes and some good curries. I wouldn't say prices are exactly cheap, but they are very affordable, especially considering the quality of the food. This location in particular is more laid-back than some of their other spots, which tend to get a bit overcrowded. Definitely a place worth hitting if you're in the area.

Rhythm

1108 W. Randolph Street 312-492-6100
Hours: Tue–Fri, 5 P.M.–2 A.M.; Sat, 7 P.M.–3 A.M.;
Sun, varies

Certainly one of the more unique bars to open here in Chicago in some time, Rhythm is a bar for the inner drummer in all of us. Along with a good selection of beer, they feature local and international drumming acts, as well as drum solo contests. On Wednesdays and Fridays they even offer free drum lessons, followed by a drum circle. Though many non-drummers might question the need for such an establishment, I'm sure drummers themselves have been dreaming of just such a place for years. Keep in mind, however, that the bar is smoke-free. In this new enlightened age in which we live, cigs and cymbals do not coexist. Call first before heading over on Sundays to make sure they're not hosting a private party.

Wishbone Restaurant

1001 W. Washington Blvd. 312-850-2663
Hours: Mon, 7 A.M.–3 P.M.; Tue–Fri, 7 A.M.–3 P.M. and
5 P.M.–10 P.M.; Sat, 8:30 A.M.–2:30 P.M. and 5 P.M.–11 P.M.;
Sun, 8:30 A.M.–2:30 P.M. and 5 P.M.–10 P.M.

This place has been around for some time and can really pack 'em in, especially for brunch on weekends. Serving up what they call "Southern Reconstruction Cooking," Wishbone offers an excellent menu, though the lunch and dinner choices are a bit limited in comparison to the breakfast menu. The jambalaya is outstanding—whether served in an omelette or on its own—and the blackened catfish is no slouch either. They also have sandwiches and plenty of vegetarian entrées to choose from, along with a handful of salads. As with Hi Ricky, prices aren't dirt cheap, but they are extremely reasonable, especially considering the gut-busting portions they dole out.

Fat Moe's Food Emporium

1159 W. Adams Street 312-733-4000
Hours: Mon–Sat, 8 A.M.–8 P.M.

This is a bustling fast-food joint that gets plenty crowded at lunchtime. In one room you can order your typical burgers and dogs and such, all of which are decent but nothing to get overly excited about. Excitement should be reserved for the deli counter in the adjacent room. Here you can get sandwiches made to order or choose from a variety of specialty subs. I used to work right around the corner from the joint, and many a time did I hop, skip, and jump through its doors. In this day of Subways and Quiznos with their anemic, imitation subs, such places as Fat Moe's are fast becoming national treasures.

4

RIVER NORTH

This is the city's "hoity-toity" section. Not only do Chicago's wealthiest folks live along Lake Shore Drive in an area known as the Gold Coast, but its premier restaurants and shops also reside here. Heavies like Bloomingdale's and Water Tower Place sit on Michigan Avenue alongside many famous restaurants. Unfor-tunately, some of the famous restaurants in River North go by names such as Hard Rock Cafe, Planet Hollywood, and Rainforest Cafe. Consequently, tourists flock here in droves, not so much inter-ested in the sights as they are in the above-mentioned restaurants and places like Navy Pier, Niketown, and the Viacom Store. Many, sadly, never see any other part of the city.

Not to knock River North. It's had its share of ups and downs—namely having all its homes and buildings burned to the ground alongside those of the Loop during the Great Fire. Only the historic Water Tower was left standing. But when the Palmers, a rich, influential family, went ahead and built their new mansion here in the 1880s, many a sycophant followed. Still, plenty of boarding houses and disreputable elements remained. This started to change after the con-struction of the Michigan Avenue Bridge in

1920. It wasn't until the late '40s, however, that the concept of the "Magnificent Mile" popped up—the term used to describe Michigan Avenue over the course of its journey north from the Loop to its end at Lake Shore Drive just past Chicago Avenue. Though streets such as Clark only a few blocks to the west remained seedy all the way into the '60s, the entire area now, of course, is sparkling clean and wholesome—with the Gallery District having replaced the strip joints. (An argument can be made that a whiff of the seedy can still be found in the hopping, pseudo-upscale bars of the Rush/Division area—though that's probably more my own opinion rather than anyone else's.) Of course, the infamous

Cabrini Green projects are only a stone's throw away, but don't worry, all those welfare cheats and their blighted buildings are being knocked to the ground and replaced by $300,000 townhouses. There is mixed-income housing being provided in the area for some Cabrini Green residents, but it would appear many of them are simply going to end up getting the shaft. Affordable housing for the poor in upscale neighborhoods is fast becoming a thing of the past in Chicago, with little being done to correct the problem. At least not while real estate prices continue to climb.

Billy Goat Tavern

430 N. Michigan Avenue 312-222-1525
Hours: Mon–Fri, 7 A.M.–2 A.M.; Sat, 10 A.M.–3 A.M.;
Sun, 11 A.M.–2 A.M.

Yes, this is the original Billy Goat Tavern immortalized by John Belushi and crew on *Saturday Night Live.* The place where the gruff men behind the counter would shout "Cheezboiger! Cheezboiger!" and "No Coke, Pepsi!" What, none of you remember that? Am I getting that old? Whatever the case, here in this dim, unevenly lit basement, you'll find your typical burgers and dogs and sandwiches, plus beer. Though drinking here is kind of like drinking in your Uncle Sal's Melrose Park basement, legendary Chicago newspapermen like Mike Royko used to swill here, and the place seems to draw aspiring journalists like Mecca draws pilgrims. If you're passing by and in the mood for a beer, you should certainly drop in.

Rand McNally Map & Travel Store

444 N. Michigan Avenue 312-321-1751
Hours: Mon, 9 A.M.–7 P.M.; Tue–Wed, 9 A.M.–6 P.M.;
Thu, 9 A.M.–7 P.M.; Fri, 9 A.M.–9 P.M.; Sat, 10 A.M.–6 P.M.;
Sun, 12 P.M.–5 P.M.

This is a small, expensive shop, but hey, it sure is cool. Here you'll find tons of guidebooks and maps, along with a number of small travel accessories such as current-adaptors and toiletry items. They also sell an impressive collection of globes—which no household should be without, if for no other reason than to grow depressed at all the places in the world you'll probably never get to visit.

Jazz Record Mart

444 N. Wabash Avenue 312-222-1467
Hours: Mon–Sat, 10 A.M.–8 P.M.; Sun, 12 P.M.–5 P.M.

If you're into jazz, this is your place. They have a huge, extensive selection of jazz CDs—new and used, as well as plenty of vinyl. You'll also find very thorough sections on blues, folk, and international music, as well as boxed sets, videos, DVDs, books and magazines. But don't come here if you're looking for the likes of Kenny G. The clerks will not only sneer, they'll probably smack you as well.

Afterwords

23 E. Illinois Street 312-464-1110
Hours: Mon–Thu, 9 A.M.–9 P.M.; Fri-Sat, 9 A.M.–11 P.M.;
Sun, 11 A.M.–6 P.M.

This new and used bookstore has a good general selection, with plenty of political books. In the basement you'll find the used stuff as well as a small cafe. The used books are displayed just as accessibly as the new ones and tend to be rather current. A good place to go if you're looking for a used copy of a book that hasn't come out in paperback yet.

Abraham Lincoln Bookshop

357 W. Chicago Avenue 312-944-3085
Hours: Mon–Sat, 9 A.M.–5 P.M.

This place is great! Though you have to be buzzed in and the general atmosphere is similar to a library what with the various portraits and paintings lining the walls, this place is not all musty and stuffy like you might expect. The staff is very friendly and helpful and the stock is incredible. If you get excited about nineteenth-century, American history—as I, admittedly, do—you'll go into raptures among the stacks. Lincoln and the Civil War are their specialities, with hundreds of books on the subjects, but you can find works on pretty much any and all topics of U.S. history, from the eighteenth century to the present. Also, if you're in the market for a replica of the Lincoln death mask—and who isn't—they have plenty to choose from, one for every budget.

Pippin's Tavern

806 N. Rush Street 312-787-5435
Hours: Sun–Fri, 11 A.M.–4 A.M.; Sat, 11 A.M.–5 A.M.

Pippin's is a rarity in this part of town: a loud yet laid-back neighborhood pub with a widely mixed clientele. Rubbing elbows in this good-natured place you'll find tony Gold Coast types, students, construction workers, off-duty chefs, and many a shade in between. And you can't beat the free baskets of popcorn. The preferred place to drink in the neighborhood.

Europa Books

832 N. State Street 312-335-9677
Hours: Mon–Fri, 8:30 A.M.–8 P.M.; Sat–Sun, 9 A.M.–8 P.M.

Here you'll encounter a wide array of magazines both domestic and foreign, as well as newspapers, foreign language books, and guidebooks. If you're European and have a hankering to see your own language in print, this is your place.

5

RIVER WEST

Much like the West Loop, River West has seen an increase in condos and residential population over the past ten years, though its former character has not been as radically altered. Instead you simply have more places to eat and hang out—as well as new construction and yuppies—than you had in the past. The neighborhood is part of what is technically known as West Town, but of course those realty folks needed a catchy new name for their little piece of pie—hence "River West" has been in use for some time, and is one of the less silly real estate monikers out there (we'll get to a few of those later in the book). The area once hosted a large immigrant Italian population. In fact, my maternal grandfather—who's ninety-one and still going strong, I must say—grew up in this area at Grand and Western. Vestiges of the Italian presence can be seen most strongly on Grand Avenue between the Milwaukee/Halsted intersection and Ogden.

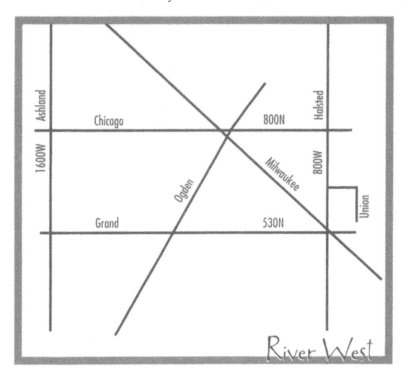

Funky Buddha Lounge

728 W. Grand Avenue 312-666-1695
Hours: Tue–Fri, 9 P.M.–2 A.M.; Sat, 9 P.M.–3 A.M.

Though I don't dance much (as in, not at all . . . unless really drunk, which is better avoided for all concerned . . .) and couldn't really imagine doing so in the Funky Buddha Lounge, I would recommend it for those who do like to dance and drink fancy drinks and such. This place has been around for years, and it is not one of those "corporatized," ultra-trendy, here-today-gone-tomorrow joints. The dance floor is actually rather small, and the interior is quite cozy, decked out in a sort of hybrid Middle-Eastern/Indian style. I've only been here a couple of times and it was for private events, so I didn't have to pay admission or full-price for drinks, which, I'm certain, saved me a bundle. However, if you're into dancing and don't mind dishing out some dough, this is definitely a unique, attractive place to hit.

Salvation Army Thrift Shop

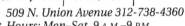

509 N. Union Avenue 312-738-4360
Hours: Mon–Sat, 9 A.M.–9 P.M.

This orderly, two-story shop is quite large, containing a good selection of furniture and various housewares on the first floor. Upstairs you'll find the clothing, as well as the "vintage boutique." This "boutique" may not rival that of your typical hipster vintage shop, but for the Salvation Army it is, I must concede, a bit "hip" indeed. On the second floor you'll also find an antique shop open Thursday through Saturday with plenty of decent items but nothing all that exciting. You won't, for example, come across the original Lincoln death mask.

Bari Foods

1120 W. Grand Avenue 312-666-0730
Hours: Mon–Sat, 8 A.M.–6:30 P.M.; Sun, 8 A.M.–1 P.M.

Right next door to D'Amato's Bakery, Bari's is a family-owned Italian grocery and butcher shop. They also make one of the most addictive, spicy Italian subs I've ever had. They must put lithium in the thing. The prosciutto and fresh mozzarella sandwich is quite good as well. Bari's also sells beer and wine; produce; plenty of imported, canned Italian delicacies; and a whole messload of pasta. The store is too small to sport any tables, but if you're passing through the area, this one of the best places to pick up a sandwich. If you've an aversion to extra-spicy food, however, you better order it up mild. These subs are so spicy they'll have you sucking air like a nitrous freak.

The Twisted Spoke

501 N. Ogden Avenue 312-666-1500
Hours: Sun–Fri, 11 A.M.–2 A.M.; Sat, 11 A.M.–3 A.M.

Ah, the Twisted Spoke. I wouldn't say I have a love/hate relationship with this place, but I am a tad ambivalent. It is sleek and well-designed, boasting a rooftop patio as well as a rotating skeleton out front astride a motor-cycle. They also serve up first-rate, very high-class bar food at reasonable prices. All the same . . . I guess what it comes down to is the last few times I went here—some years back now—it was for the Tuesday $2 pints of Guiness special, which a friend of mine, a trans-planted Englishman, viewed as a weekly gift from Heaven. There were never more than four of us, and we never seemed to be there for all that long, yet our tabs were invariably over a hundred bucks. It's one of those deals where you're not expecting to spend a lot of money, and yet end up spending a ton. The betrayal one feels on such occasions is always far greater than the pleasure one receives on those rare evenings when you spend considerably less than you had intended while still having a great time (and paying your fair share). In hindsight, of course, my growing dissatisfac-tion with the Twisted Spoke was misplaced—it was our own prodigious thirsts that pauperized us on those Tuesdays. Still, attending this place does seem a bit like throwing money down a well. No matter how much you think you're going to spend, it always turns out to be more. Yet as long as you are aware of this, the Twisted Spoke is indeed a fine place to imbibe but especially to eat. Just don't run up a tab.

Black Market Chicago

XXX *1105 W. Chicago Avenue, 3rd Floor 312-421-9690*
Hours: Tue–Sat, 12 P.M.–8 P.M.

For the leather fetishist in all of us, Black Market—recently transplanted from its long residency in Wicker Park—provides all your S&M needs as well as lingerie, vibrators, sex toys, lubricants, etc. Despite the foreboding merchandise, this is a very friendly shop. They can also outfit the well-dressed goth and provide plenty of printed literature if they're looking to specialize in a particular S&M field.

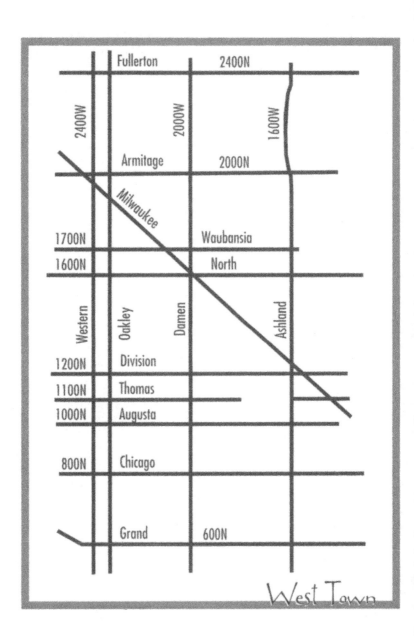

6

WEST TOWN

West Town is one of the more interesting areas of the city—and probably one of the neighborhoods in which you'll be spending quite a bit of time. Originally a suburb of Chicago containing some impressive mansions, the area started declining around the 1920s. By the '40s it was a Polish ghetto. Nelson Algren wrote about this area in *The Man with the Golden Arm*. In fact, a portion of Division Street was called Polish Broadway due to all the bars and clubs along its length. Despite the heavy concentration of Poles, however, West Town is made up of several ethnicities and neighborhoods. Wicker Park, Bucktown, East Village, Ukrainian Village, Logan Square, River West—all are within West Town. Over the past decade these neighborhoods have gone through intense gentrification, with Bucktown foremost among them. My earliest memory of Bucktown is not exactly pleasant. Years back when I was still a teenager and self-proclaimed "punk rocker," some friends and I were attacked without warning by a gleeful band of youthful white hardasses. The chances of this happening now are all but nil. Unless, perhaps, you manage to tap the bumper of the SUV in front of you while parallel parking.

Before you know it you may find yourself under attack by a well-groomed yuppie family and their yellow lab. Yes, though vestiges of the Mexican community are still present, Bucktown is a yuppie haven. They've bought houses and condos throughout the entire neighborhood. The shops are mostly expensive boutiques, and the restaurants are of the glitzy, trendy variety.

Wicker Park is becoming very similar. Right next to Bucktown, Wicker's main intersection of Milwaukee, Damen, and North used to be a desolate, garbage-strewn eyesore only some thirteen years ago. Now the large Mexican and Polish communities that resided here—as well as the masses of artists—are being pushed out in favor of strip malls, condos, and yuppies.

The artists started the decline, as usual. Back in the '80s, space was dirt cheap in the neighborhood, but as more and more artists moved in, the inevitable slew of students and assorted hipsters followed. And yes, I was one of them. Except for a few short stints in New Orleans, I lived in Wicker Park from 1991 to 1997. The neighborhood has drastically changed since I first arrived—both in its ethnic makeup and the character of its shops and eateries, but what else is new? This has been happening since the beginning of the city.

The other neighborhoods, such as East Village, are yielding much more slowly to change, but change is indeed making itself felt. More and more the young "artistes" are being driven into the cheaper, heavily Mexican areas, and the Mexicans, in turn, are being forced further west. Even Ukrainian Village—a respectable bastion of old world Ukrainians and Polish—has been inundated. Years back a Brazilian friend of mine was looking for an apartment in the area. Though he's as white as George Bush, he ended up using his girlfriend's last name in dealing with landlords. Somehow the name of Pinto wasn't opening the right doors for him. That, however, isn't much of a problem these days, as you see plenty of young, mixed-race, hipster couples living in the neighborhood.

Now you may be wondering why I've lumped all these

separate neighborhoods into the convenient heading of West Town. The reason is simple. The boundaries of these areas are not too firmly fixed—at least not in the minds of the residents. In the course of one night's carousal in West Town, you may very well wander into every single one of these neighborhoods as you flit from place to place. Therefore, to impose some sort of order to all this, I've decided to lump businesses together not by neighborhood, but by street. Milwaukee Avenue, for example, is one of West Town's main arteries. It enters West Town in East Village and passes from Wicker Park and Bucktown into Logan Square (the latter an area I will deal with separately as it is "psychologically"—if not technically—outside of West Town). Chicago Avenue, on the other hand, enters in East Village and continues through Ukrainian Village, never hitting Wicker Park proper. Yet despite this, Chicago Avenue is as much a part of the Wicker Park "experience" as Milwaukee Avenue itself.

All right then, I've been rambling on for far too long. But that's okay because as I said at the beginning of this lengthy opus, you'll probably be spending a lot of time here. This region is second only to the Belmont/Clark area up north as Chicago's premier hipster shopping district. You'll find plenty of vintage shops and book and record stores, and an immense slew of bars, clubs and restaurants. Here also are plenty of Mexican discount shops and taquerias, as well as a number of Polish joints. It's not very hard to have a good time here. Much like that silken-voiced president of Men's Wearhouse, I guarantee it.

Milwaukee Avenue

Entering West Town in East Village, you'll find one side of Milwaukee taken up by very well-kept, low-rise projects while various upscale, hipster businesses hold court across the street. Past the big intersection at Ashland and Division, you hit Wicker Park proper. Gentrification generally hasn't spread here yet; tacky furniture shops and dollar stores are in the majority. Soon enough, however, you're smack dab in a gentrification jamboree as you approach the six-corner intersection at Damen and North. On weekend nights this place is hopping, especially after 2am when everyone is headed to their favorite after-hours bar. North of the intersection used to be a quiet, industrial area. No more. Insidious strip malls and condos have sprouted up, and with them businesses like Blockbuster Video. After the intersection at Western, Milwaukee heads into Logan Square, where you'll find one of my all-time favorite thrift stores—Village Discount Outlet (written up in the Logan Square section).

Ark Thrift Shop

1302 N. Milwaukee Avenue 773-862-5011
Hours: Mon–Thu: 10 A.M.–6 P.M.; Fri, 10 A.M.–5 P.M.
(summer) 10 A.M.–2 P.M. (winter); Sun, 11 A.M.–5 P.M.

Ah, the Ark empire. You'll find a few of these shops throughout the city. This location is a good place to find cheap furniture. The clothes selection is nothing special, but the bargain basement is always good for a browse. Here you'll find the really cheap stuff, from chairs and tables to exercise equipment and only slightly soiled mattresses.

Gaia Movement Resale Shop

1318 N. Milwaukee Avenue 312-645-0806
Hours: Mon–Thu, 11 A.M.–8 P.M.; Fri–Sat, 11 A.M.–7 P.M.;
Sun, 10 A.M.–6 P.M.

I'm afraid I don't know much about the GAIA Movement. About all I know is that one day their bright green drop boxes started popping up all over the city. I've put clothes in them too. That's about the extent of it, except that they then sell these clothes to raise funds to do good things in the world. So perhaps if you wander into their store you may actually buy a piece of clothing that I used to own, the proceeds of which will help the planet much more than I ever have. Or maybe not. I'm not sure they would actually sell my castoffs in their store, for there's some very nice stuff here. Most of the clothes are even somewhat hipsterish, albeit conservatively so. The same can be said about the shoes, their collection of which, I brazenly declare, is the best I've ever seen in an "institutional" resale shop. So though I don't know much about the GAIA Movement, I do know that this particular store carries some high quality threads. If you need some stylish, more functional wear rather than casual, out-on-the-town duds, this is a very good place to visit.

Wonderland Multivintage

 1339 N. Milwaukee Avenue 773-235-3110
Hours: Mon–Fri, 12 P.M.–7 P.M.; Sat, 12 P.M.–6 P.M.;
Sun, 12 P.M.–5 P.M.

This dim shop carries a wide variety of pop culture icons and old toys, much of it brand name-type stuff. For example, you won't find too many stuffed animals that aren't readily identifiable, whether its Dino the Dinosaur from *The Flintstones,* Heathcliff the cat, or the Tasmanian Devil. You'll also find an extensive collection of old fast food chain "special offer" glasses bearing the images of Superman and assorted others. There's plenty of other stuff too, from books to old baseball bats and mitts, much of it hailing from the '60s and '70s. This place will come in especially handy if you've been attempting to assemble an army of plastic Smurfs. They probably have enough of them for an entire battalion, which you can use to conquer and dominate a village of limbless Fisher Price people.

Una Mae's Freak Boutique

 1422 N. Milwaukee Avenue 773-276-7002
Hours: Mon–Fri, 12 P.M.–8 P.M.; Sat, 11 A.M.–8 P.M.;
Sun, 11 A.M.–7 P.M.

Despite the name, you won't find this place to be unusually freaky, but you will find plenty of decently priced, good quality vintage clothing for women and men, as well as accessories made by local designers. They do have some never-worn stuff with original price tags. That doesn't mean, of course, that you can purchase these items for the original cost. Life isn't that easy. This is a nicely appointed little shop.

Brown Elephant Resale Shop

1459 N. Milwaukee Avenue 773-252-8801
Hours: Open every day, 11 A.M.–6 P.M.

There are a few Brown Elephant resale shops in Chicago, with proceeds benefiting the Howard Brown Health Center, and they're by far the best "institutional" resale establishments you're ever apt to see. This particular shop is almost swank, looking more like a vintage shop rather than a Salvation Army or Village Thrift store. Here you'll find good quality clothing, a few nice pieces of furniture and some housewares, and plenty of albums, CDs, books, videos, and DVDs. As for the music, books, and films, none of the titles leap out at you, but a browse will turn up several decent items.

Myopic Books

1468 N. Milwaukee Avenue 773-862-4882
Hours: Mon–Fri, 11 A.M.–1 A.M.; Sat, 11 A.M.–1 A.M.;
Sun, 11 A.M.–10 P.M.

One of the best used book stores in Wicker Park, and certainly the most enduring, though it's switched locations a few times over the years. Open nice and late, the atmosphere here is very laid-back and comfortable, even if it is a tight squeeze between shelves. Comprised of three levels, Myopic offers a good general selection of stuff. The fiction section in particular is big and thorough. They also have plenty of art books, and a decent mishmash of history titles. This in addition to a large smattering of what they delicately refer to as "Fuck" books.

Recycle Men's & Women's Designer Resale

1474 N. Milwaukee Avenue 773-645-1900
Hours: Mon–Sat, 11 A.M.–7 P.M.; Sun, 11 A.M.–5 P.M.

This spacious shop carries a large quantity of mint-condition clothing and footwear. The range in styles is quite large, from funky to downright conservative. In fact, if you're like me and try to avoid wearing a suit whenever possible, this is a great place to get one. The prices are generally up above the sixty-dollar mark, but they're in great shape and should last for several years worth of weddings and funerals.

El Chino

1505 N. Milwaukee Avenue 773-772-1905
Hours: Sun–Fri, 11 A.M.–4:30 A.M.; Sat, 11 A.M.–5 A.M.

Good old El Chino. What makes this place so popular is its willingness to remain open after 4 A.M. Once Nick's across the street starts itching to kick its patrons out for the night, El Chino reaps the benefits. Their food is, for the most part, nothing special—but it is cheap. While the chorizo tastes unlike any I've ever had—and I don't mean that in a positive way—the chips and salsa are very good, and the chicken quesadillas are pretty tasty as well. Oddly enough, however, I don't think the chicken quesadillas have any actual cheese in them. Granted, my powers of analysis are always skewed when I'm there—there's no real reason to eat there if you're sober—but I swear that's the case. Go figure.

U.S. #1

1509 N. Milwaukee Avenue 773-489-9428
Hours: Open Every day 11 A.M.–7 P.M.

No, this isn't the official store of the Bush Administration, nor is it owned by Lee Greenwood or sponsored by the Fox News Channel. Those of you looking for Bill O'Reilly bath oils will have to go elsewhere. What you'll find here instead are used jeans and leather jackets, for both men and woman, and miscellaneous shirts and blouses. The prices aren't cheap, but the merchandise is very high quality.

Salvation Army Thrift Store

1515 N. Milwaukee Avenue 773-489-5194
Hours: Mon–Sat, 9 A.M.–9 P.M.

This Salvation Army branch is spacious but not particularly rewarding. You'll find a basic selection of clothes and shoes here along with dishes, knickknacks, and a bit of furniture. I should mention, however, that the books are worth picking through, as you can occasionally find something decent.

Nick's

1516 N. Milwaukee Avenue 773-252-1155
Hours: Sun–Fri, 4 P.M.–4 A.M.; Sat, 4 P.M.–5 A.M.

Nick's occupies the site of what used to be Club Dreamerz. Dreamerz was a bit of a legend in its time, yet even so you're not likely to find too many people—myself included—who are proud to admit that they used to hang out there all the time. Nick's doesn't have this problem, I imagine. Having been forced out of its ancestral home in Lincoln Park, Nick's was one of the first wave of more upscale joints that began to hit Wicker Park years back. What was once a rather rundown bar with nasty bathrooms is now a very attractive, well-kept joint. Pool tables have filled the dance floor and the DJs have been replaced with a jukebox, but the place still fills up after 4 A.M. on Saturdays. Only now the crowd has a little less ennui and a lot more money. This is good in a way, as the amount of near-strangers trying to bum drinks off you pretty much disappeared with the demise of Dreamerz. A beer garden is open during the warmer months, but unlike the old days it's no longer decorated with tombstones and huge, stark paintings of naked zombies. Oh, well.

Reckless Records

1532 N. Milwaukee Avenue 773-235-3727
Hours: Mon–Sat, 10 A.M.–10 P.M.; Sun, 10 A.M.–8 P.M.

 One of two stores the highly respected Reckless chain keeps in Chicago. Here you'll find an outstanding selection of new, used, and rare CDs, vinyl, cassettes, videos, and DVDs, as well as a smattering of music mags and 'zines. Reckless also offers the best prices in the city if you're looking to sell off any old albums.

Big Horse

1558 N. Milwaukee Avenue 773-384-0043
Hours: Sun–Fri, 10 A.M.–2 A.M., Sat, 10 A.M.–3 A.M.

Big Horse combines the best of the old Wicker Park in one cramped, smoky little den. In front is a genuine Mexican taqueria serving up burritos and nachos and all sorts of goodies, while in back you can drink anything from a small selection of imports to your typical cheap corporate brew while watching locals whale away on their instruments at the other end of the room. You can never be sure just what caliber of band might be playing here. You get anything from seasoned veterans doing a knockoff show for fun to kids who have never had an audience beyond their boyfriends and girlfriends. Though bands started playing here only about ten years ago, this place quickly become an institution.

Earwax

1561 N. Milwaukee Avenue 773-772-4019
Hours: Mon, 12 P.M.–12 A.M.; Tue–Thu, 4 P.M.–12 A.M.,
Fri–Sun, 12 P.M.–12 A.M.

 Earwax quickly developed into a Wicker Park institution upon its arrival in the neighborhood over a decade ago—and has managed to retain that status despite the heavy competition that has sprung up around it over the years. Though there are other coffee shops a stone's throw away in either direction, only

Earwax really needs to be mentioned. The other places are fine and all, but Earwax definitely stands out. Primarily a coffeehouse serving up good grub (I even had a decent mufaletta here once), this joint also serves as a book and music store, not to mention a video rental outlet. The selection of books and CDs is small but very good, while their stock of videos and DVDs is exceptional. Everything from hard-to-find documentaries to foreign films and '70s exploitation— as well as high-quality Hollywood fare—can be found here. And you don't need a membership to rent, just a credit card and driver's license.

The Note

1565 N. Milwaukee Avenue 773-489-0011
Hours: Sun–Tue, 10 P.M.–4 A.M.; Wed–Fri, 8 P.M.–4 A.M.;
Sat, 8 P.M.–5 A.M.

The Note has come a long way from its days as a jazz juke-joint on Armitage Avenue. Since moving to the Flat Iron Building some years back, it began hosting jazz and funk acts as well as swing bands. Though such acts still appear, they now offer a heavy dose of hip hop, with open mic nights a couple times a week, as well as straight-ahead rock bands. One thing hasn't changed—it still gets very crowded after the 2 A.M. bars close.

Double Door

1572 N. Milwaukee Avenue 773-489-3160
Hours: Varies depending on show. Doors usually open at
8 or 9 P.M.

Converted from an old redneck bar and takeout liquor joint, this is Wicker Park's only large venue for local and national bands. From relatively unknown locals to legends such as Pere Ubu, a wide gamut of bands play here. Drink prices are high, but they do occasionally have specials. Downstairs you'll find a whole slew of pool tables, while in a little nook up a small flight of stairs from the main room, you'll find a comfortable lounging area. The interior of Double Door is very well done, and if you can kick back here on a night when it's not too crowded, it's a very comfortable place to see a band.

The House of Monsters

 1579 N. Milwaukee Avenue 2nd Floor 773-292-0980
Hours: Sat, 12 P.M.–6 P.M.; Sun, 12 P.M.–5 P.M.

Located in the Flat Iron Building, this place stocks an amazing collection of sci-fi and horror films on VHS, DVD, and even laser disc. We're talking thousands of films, from old classics like *Mr. Sardonicus* and *Devil Girl from Mars* to more modern masterpieces like *Billy the Kid Vs. Dracula* and, of course, *I Dismember Mama*. But films aren't the only thing this place stocks. You'll also find a large collection of Japanese monster toys and model kits, books, posters, and masks. This is definitely one of the coolest shops in Chicago.

Occult Bookstore

 1579 N. Milwaukee Avenue 3rd Floor 773-292-0995
Hours: Mon–Thu, 12 P.M.–7 P.M.; Fri–Sat,
12 P.M.–8 P.M.; Sun, 12 P.M.–6 P.M.

This venerable institution has been around since 1915 in various locations, and have now set up shop in the big old Flat Iron Building. Here you'll find an outstanding collection of books on the arcane, metaphysical, and, of course, the occult. They also sell a large collection of publications along with incense, candles, and various talismans and crystals and such.

Irazu

 1865 N. Milwaukee Avenue 773-252-5687
Hours: Mon–Sat, 10 A.M.–9 P.M.

I used to live right near Irazu when it was a cramped little carry-out joint serving up their special Costa Rican burritos and specialities. The wait could sometimes be long then, and only got worse when they spruced the place up and added an outdoor patio. It is still well worth it, however, both in price and quality. Plus, it's BYOB—something that always endears me to a place.

Threads Etc.

2327 N. Milwaukee Avenue 773-276-6411
Hours: Mon–Sat, 11 A.M.–7 P.M.; Sun, 11 A.M.–5 P.M.

This is a fine resale/vintage shop with plenty of goods for both men and women. In the old days standard shirts, pants, and jeans filled most of the racks, along with plenty of footwear and a selection of CDs and cassettes. Now they also carry furniture, including a number of good-quality mattresses. The staff are friendly and more than willing to let you know if there's a special sale in effect.

ASHLAND AVENUE

Over the course of its journey through West Town, Ashland retains the same commercial character it has had for years. Here on this broad avenue you'll find mundane mom-and-pop shops, many of them Mexican-owned. From Grand Avenue to North Avenue, however, there are a few places to check out.

Betty's Blue Star Lounge

1600 W. Grand Avenue 312-243-1699
Hours: Sun–Fri, 7 A.M.–4 A.M.; Sat, 11 A.M.–5 A.M.

Up until fairly recently, Betty's was an unremarkable neighborhood bar catering to the old-timer locals. Hipsters did make appearances, but only after 2 A.M. when there was no better option. And then the place would soak you, upping the price of their drinks to exorbitant levels. A couple of desperate friends and I once even bought a case of Old Style to go around

3 A.M. I can't remember the exact price, but it was definitely over thirty bucks—and this was years ago. Betty's will still fork over beer to go, but it has now made the transition to a hipster bar. DJs spin nightly, with most nights offering a heavy dose of hip hop and house music, though they also feature rock and '80s nights as well. Bands occasionally play here also.

Wax Addict

1014 N. Ashland Avenue 773-772-9930
Hours: Tue–Sat, 12 P.M.–10 P.M.; Sun, 12 P.M.–6 P.M.

If you're into serious dance music and deejaying, this is a great place to go for local, national, and international releases. From classic disco and funk to hip hop, techno, and plain old pop, this place has it covered.

Revolution Books

1103 N. Ashland Avenue 773-489-0930
Hours: Tue–Fri, 2 A.M.–7 P.M.; Sat, 11 A.M.–7 P.M.

What every city needs, a good leftist, agit-prop book shop. This store—staffed entirely by volunteers—features plenty of works on the wonders of socialism and the evils of corporate capitalism. A fine place to gift shop for that know-it-all right-winger in the family.

Dusty Groove

1120 N. Ashland Avenue 773-342-5800
Hours: Mon–Sun, 10 A.M.–8 P.M.

This well-stocked record store is a great place to hit if you're looking for jazz and world music. They sell tons of old vinyl along with CDs, and also have good current selections of hip hop, acid jazz, and various "drum & bass" compilations. Amid the reasonably priced vinyl you'll find plenty of old Latin and African albums.

La Pasadita

1132 N. Ashland Avenue 773-278-2130
Hours: Sun–Thur, 9:30 A.M.–1:30am; Fri–Sat,
9:30 A.M.–3 A.M.

This place serves up the best burritos in town. In particular, their barbacoa burritos are phenomenal. Though there are two other La Pasaditas right nearby— one a few doors down and one across the street—I'm afraid I've never felt the need to sample the other two. I've meant to, but then the thought of that barbacoa burrito awaiting me draws me right back into ol' bright yeller. Not very adventurous, I know, but I just can't help myself. This is definitely a place to hit.

CHICAGO AVENUE

The East Village section of Chicago Avenue is still primarily Mexican, with furniture shops and various other such practical establishments. This continues past Ashland up to Damen Avenue. Now you're starting to get into Ukrainian Village.

Demar's

1701 W. Chicago Avenue 312-666-4317
Hours: Mon–Sat, 5:30 A.M.–7 P.M.; Sun, 5:30 A.M.–6 P.M.

Something that is fast becoming a rarity in many parts of West Town: a genuine, dirt-cheap diner. From ridiculously low-priced breakfasts to edible sandwiches and dinner specials, Demar's is a no-frills, authentic relic of what is fast being replaced by expensive, stylized versions of the same.

American Thrift Store

1718 W. Chicago Avenue 312-243-4343
Hours: Mon–Sat, 11 A.M.–7 P.M.; Sun, 11 A.M.–5 P.M.

Though it can be hot and muggy inside, you'll find this a well-kept, orderly shop. Hanging from the many

racks are all sorts of incredibly cheap, basic clothing.
For items like T-shirts, sweatshirts, and button-down
shirts, this is your place. (But I must say the pricing is a
little odd. I once bought a sweatshirt here for $1.88.
Not exactly a figure you're used to seeing at a resale
shop.)

Tecalitlan

 1814 W. Chicago Avenue 773-384-4285
Hours: Mon–Thu, 9 A.M.–12 A.M.; Fri–Sun, 7 A.M.–3 A.M.

This Mexican restaurant not only provides a carry-out
station to give you easy access to their excellent burritos and such, but they also have a spacious dining
room and full-service bar. Their prices increased several years back when they remodeled, but they're still
pretty reasonable and the food is worth it.

Cleo's

1935 W. Chicago Avenue 312-243-5600
Hours: Mon–Fri, 5 P.M.–2 A.M.; Sat, 5 P.M.–3 A.M.;
Sun, 11 A.M.–2 A.M.

 This is one of the old wave of "newcomers" to the area,
meaning it arrived sometime in the mid-nineties
(you'll have to forgive my memory) along with a slew
of other joints hoping to cash in on the vibrant
nightlife of the area, which was now attracting more
and more non-"artiste" residents. Cleo's was a comfy,
attractive, good-natured little place that served up
some decent bar food. It never got too crowded even
when it hosted the occasional band. The place seemed
to have much bigger aspirations, however, for their ads
would always feature some scantily clad bimbo, as if
they were hoping to draw in a crowd of martini-drink-
ing, hi-energy clubbie sorts. Therefore I assumed they
would soon fail like many a similar new establishment.
Cleo's, however, finally seemed to accept itself for what
it was and began to settle comfortably into its role as
an attractive, good-natured little neighborhood joint.

Their bar food has gone from decent to high class, with their pizza selections in particular quite good. This is a great place to hit if you simply want to kick back and down a few without having to deal with any attitude or preening. They also feature works by local artists, so you can take in a bit of culture along with the suds and food.

Atomix Coffee Shop

1957 W. Chicago Avenue 312-666-2649
Hours: Mon–Fri, 7 A.M.–10 P.M.; Sat–Sun, 9 A.M.–10 P.M.

This is one of the new wave of newcomers to the area, which simply means they arrived after the first edition of this book was published in 1999. Done up in a sort of space-age retro sixties style, here along with the joe you'll find a decent selection of food, with plenty of vegetarian fare. They also offer internet hookups.

Kasia's Polish Deli

2101 W. Chicago Avenue 773-486-6163
Hours: Mon–Sun, 9 A.M.–6 P.M.

If you've got a hankering for some great pierogis or other Polish dishes, this is the place to go. They've got a huge, mouth-watering selection sitting under glass just waiting to slide down your grubby little gullet. The place isn't big enough for a dining area so you'll have to take your goodies and go, but if you speak Polish, make sure to chat awhile with the neighborhood ladies.

Old Lviv

2228 W. Chicago Avenue 773-772-7250
Hours: closed Mon; Tue–Sat, 11 A.M.–8 P.M.;
Sun, 11 A.M.–7 P.M.

Been looking for a Ukrainian buffet? If you haven't, you should've been. This tiny little restaurant will have you begging for mercy after a couple trips to the buffet table. For very reasonable prices you can get your fill of sausages and potatoes as well chicken drumsticks, pork, and cabbage. Memories of the famine in the Soviet Union in the 1930s apparently die hard.

Sak's Ukrainian Village Restaurant

 2301 W. Chicago Avenue 773-278-4445
Hours: Tue–Sun, 11:30 A.M.–10 P.M.

This homey joint is both a bar and restaurant, with the kitchen serving up the usual hearty Ukrainian fare— heavy on the meat, cabbage, and potatoes. The prices are cheap, the food is "rib-sticking," and you've even got a whole wall of Ukrainian art to admire. This is a very friendly place. The bar, by the way, stays open till 2 A.M. on Fridays and 3 A.M. on Saturdays.

AUGUSTA BOULEVARD

Augusta is primarily residential, and still heavily Mexican. A quiet, pleasant street, it hosts a few bars east of Damen before entering Ukrainian Village.

Clubfoot Lounge

1824 W. Augusta Boulevard 773-489-0379
Hours: Sun–Fri, 8 P.M.–2 A.M.; Sat, 8 P.M.–3 A.M.

Definitely one of my favorite bars. There's never a cover, a DJ spins every night, and the atmosphere and crowd are consistently laid-back and friendly. It doesn't usually get overcrowded either, so most of the time you can find a seat or get a turn at the pool table. Owners Chuck and Laurie have been involved in the Chicago music scene for years. Chuck played in legendary Chicago punk bands The Defoliants and No Empathy, while Laurie has DJ'd at various clubs for as long as I can remember. An amusing array of punk and new wave memorabilia—from T-shirts to newspaper clippings—lines the walls, and various odd toys perch behind the bar. All this and weekday drink specials as well. A must-visit place.

Leona's Restaurant

1936 W. Augusta Boulevard 773-292-4300
Hours: Mon–Thu, 11 A.M.–11 P.M.; Fri–Sat, 11 A.M.–1 A.M.;
Sun, 12 P.M.–11 P.M.

For my money, Leona's has the best thin-crust pizza in Chicago. It is the standard by which I judge all other pizzas. And all other pizzas usually come up short of the Leona's standard. A Chicago institution for decades, Leona's now has restaurants serving most of the city's neighborhoods and many suburbs beyond. The Wicker Park location incorporates an actual brick three-flat into its facade and is a casual, convivial place to drink and fill up your guts. In addition to the pizza you can get anything from seafood dishes to burgers. The prices aren't bargains, but the portions and side dishes are large and the food is always excellent. Their specialty sandwiches deserve a mention as well. They are huge and very tasty.

Innertown Pub

1935 W. Thomas Avenue 773-235-9795
Hours: Sun–Fri, 3 P.M.–2 A.M.; Sat, 3 P.M.–3 A.M.

Back in the days when I used to go out all the time, the Innertown Pub was my favorite Chicago bar, and it still, I must say, lingers pleasantly—if a bit murkily—in my memory. Though prices have gone up a bit over the years, the place still has the look and feel of a rundown Wisconsin roadhouse and you can still get domestic pints for only two dollars. Though the place is predominantly frequented by local art slobs, it does have a fairly well mixed clientele, with big crowds practically every night of the week. Attitude is nonexistent; it truly is a place where you can park yourself at the bar not knowing a soul and be deep in conversation only minutes later. Not that the conversation itself will always be that deep—or coherent—hey, at least it's friendly. The jukebox is good, and the pool tables, though not so good, are fiercely contested for each and every night. The female bartenders—and I suppose the male ones too—are also highly appealing to the eyes. They're not shy about pouring out a free shot or two now and then either. On many nights you can find the owner—who has been aptly described as an ancient Wayne Newton lookalike—hanging about. On such nights you ladies may even attract his attention. Having him hit on you is a dubious honor, to be sure, but it is part of the "female" Innertown experience. Enjoy.

DIVISION STREET

Division Street starts hopping just past the intersection of Ashland and Milwaukee. From here to Western you'll find a number of hipster shops and eateries holding court with the remnants of old Polish bars and Mexican tire shops that used to proliferate on this street. Unlike Chicago Avenue, which has changed little in the past decade, Division has been glitzed up considerably—even sporting a small strip mall. Though its appearance can be a bit disconcerting to someone who remembers the way it used to look in the early days of the hipster invasion of the area, you certainly can't complain about the absence of empty bottles that used to litter the sidewalks. No, it is no longer possible for one of your drunken buddies to do a spirited "bottle dance" down the length of an entire block—which, it goes without saying, is not a bad thing.

Arandas

1555 W. Division Street 773-252-1505
Hours: Open every day, 8 A.M.–3 A.M.

Yet another Wicker Park taqueria, this one is particularly handy for late-night eats. The burritos are good, and though I've always been too squeamish to try it,

I'm told the menudo is quite tasty. Strangely enough, the horchata is particularly good here. I'm at a loss as to why. Perhaps they clean the machine more often than usual . . . or, conversely, maybe they don't clean the machine as often as they should. . . .

Lilly Vallente

1746 W. Division Street 773-645-1537
Hours: Tue–Sat, 12 P.M.–8 P.M.; Sun, 12 P.M.–7 P.M.

A relative newcomer to Division, this place is one of the better vintage shops in the area, from the elegant, dim—dare I say somewhat "Victorian"—decor of its interior to its merchandise. Here you can find both men and women's clothing—everything from jeans and simple dresses to genuine fur coats—as well as a small collection of household items, candles, and a few bicycles.

Gold Star

1755 W. Division Street 773-227-8700
Hours: Sun–Fri, 4 P.M.–2 A.M.; Sat, 4 P.M.–3 A.M.

This place has been around forever, as the subdued, art-deco interior indicates. This is a nice, low-key place to knock back a few or shoot some pool. It usually doesn't get too crowded and the prices are decent.

Phyllis' Musical Inn

1800 W. Division Street 773-486-9862
Hours: Mon–Fri, 3 P.M.–2 A.M.; Sat, 3 P.M.–3 A.M.;
Sun, 1 P.M.–2 A.M.

Another Chicago institution, Phyllis' has been in the same family since the '60s. Nothing special to look at, Phyllis' is small and comfy, with a tiny stage. Many of the bands that play here are unknown—indeed, many play their first gigs here—but the quality level is usually decent at least. If you're a hockey fan in general or a Blackhawk fan in particular, this is the place to watch games. The owner and his cohorts are fanatics. Music is featured every night. And hey, how many joints host a weekly "Bike Messenger Night"?

The Smoke Daddy

1804 W. Division Street 773-772-6656
Hours: Mon–Wed, 11:30 A.M.–12 A.M.; Thu–Sun, 11:30 A.M.–1 A.M.

This colorful little joint has been around for nearly a decade now, serving up tasty barbecue sandwiches and ribs while hosting free bands every night of the week. Prices are decent and the food is good. The barbecue platters are especially worth your while.

Leo's Lunchroom

1809 W. Division Street 773-276-6509
Hours: Closed Mon, Tue–Sun, 8 A.M.–10 P.M.

Famous throughout Wicker Park if not the rest of Chicago, Leo's Lunchroom is a funky, hopping, tiny joint serving up a great selection of mostly veggie entrées. From sandwiches and chili to more elaborate fare, the quality is always excellent. The menu changes frequently and the atmosphere is very laid back and still a bit bohemian.

Moonshine

1824 W. Division Street 773-862-8686
Hours: Mon–Wed, 12 P.M.–10 P.M.; Thu–Sun, 12 P.M.–11 P.M.

Part of the new wave of Division Street establishments, Moonshine is an airy, laid-back eatery serving up high-class diner and bar fare. Their shrimp po' boy, in particular, is definitely worth sampling. Live music is also featured, and, best of all, you can avoid racking up a huge bill since it's BYOB. Clay jugs are also welcome.

Weekend

1919 W. Division Street 773-347-5768
Hours: Mon–Sat, 11 A.M.–8 P.M.; Sun, 12 P.M.–6 P.M.

Ever wished you could fulfill both your music and soap needs in one convenient location? Now you can (okay, I guess you can do the same thing at Wal Mart, but they have crap music). This tiny shop features a small but decent selection of vinyl and CDs as well as several bars of specialty soaps. A DJ station in the corner even provides tunes to enhance your shopping experience. Definitely one of the more unique concept joints to spring up in awhile.

Jinx

1928 W. Division Street 773-645-3667
Hours: Mon, 4 P.M.–11 P.M.; Tue–Sun, 11 A.M.–11 P.M.

This small, dim, low-frills coffee shop is a decent place to sit and drink your joe. You won't find baskets of muffins and goodies on display, though they do serve sandwiches and make one hell of a mean chocolate milkshake. And if I may say so, their black cat logo is one of the coolest business logos in the city.

Rock-a-Tiki

1942 W. Division Street 773-384-8454
Hours: Tue–Fri, 7 P.M.–2 A.M.; Sat, 7 P.M.–3 A.M.;
Sun, 8 P.M.–2 A.M.

This club is exactly what you think it is—a tiki bar. Heavy on the bamboo and lanterns, Rock-a-Tiki is a good place to visit if you're in the mood for a kitschy little excursion but don't feel like traveling to Disney World to further line the pockets of that low-down rat (though I still can fondly remember that parrot chorus: "In the Tiki-Tiki-Tiki-Tiki-Tiki room, in the Tiki-Tiki-Tiki-Tiki-Tiki room. . ."). The restaurant is open up to a half-hour before closing and they serve up some interesting seafood dishes, though, sadly, no Polynesian hot dogs. But let's face it—you're really here for the drinks. They have dozens of those, from traditional fare like hurricanes and daiquiris to house specialties like Pirate's Grog and the charmingly named Suffering Bastard. This place isn't cheap, but if you're in the mood for this type of joint and don't mind spending some money, it's well worth it.

D & D Liquor

2006 W. Division Street 773-252-3012
Hours: Sun–Thu, 9 A.M.–1 A.M.; Fri–Sat, 9 A.M.–2 A.M.

One of my favorite liquor stores, though not many people seem to agree with me. Okay, so the six packs are all about a dollar more expensive here than anywhere else, but they have an outstanding selection for a neighborhood shop that makes most of its money selling malt liquor and Old Style to winos. The wine selection is also large with plenty of good deals. I very much miss the time when I lived only two short blocks from here. My liver doesn't, but I do.

Letizia's Natural Bakery

2144 W. Division Street 773-342-1011
Hours: Mon–Fri, 6 A.M.–11 P.M.; Sat–Sun,
6:30 A.M.–11 P.M.

This is a comfortable, attractive place to have some baked goodies and coffee. They also offer pizza and a large selection of very good paninis. Prices aren't cheap, but the quality is first-rate. Both the outdoor seating area in front and the patio in back are very pleasant places in which to pass some time.

NORTH AVENUE

After crossing under the Kennedy Expressway heading west, you are in Wicker Park. Many of the old ethnic businesses on North Avenue have been replaced with hipster versions, but you'll still find a smattering of ethnic groceries, bars, and other shops intermingled. These are much more prevalent west of the six-corner intersection at Milwaukee and Damen, especially as you approach Western Avenue.

Bucktown Pub

1658 W. Cortland Street 773-394-9898
Hours: Sun–Fri, 12 P.M.–2 A.M.; Sat, 12 P.M.–3 A.M.

Though no longer in its original location, the Bucktown Pub has been around since the early '70s. Low-key and comfortable, this is the ultimate neighborhood bar for both old-timers and newcomers alike. Plenty of old cartoons and artwork cover the walls, and you can drink Bucktown Lager on the cheap. Of course Bucktown Lager tastes suspiciously like Special Export, but so what? This is a cool little place to kick back in.

Quimby's Qveer Store

1854 W. North Avenue 773-342-0910
Hours: Mon–Fri, 12 P.M.–10 P.M.; Sat, 11 A.M.–10 P.M.;
Sun, 12 P.M.–6 P.M.

Quimby's is a member of that fraternity of establishments that opened in the early days of the Wicker Park hipster settlement and developed into an institution. Though they had to move from their original digs over on Damen, the store is still one of the best of its kind. Here in this bright, spacious location you'll find a gigantic slew of fanzines and underground comics, offbeat fiction and non-fiction, and several chap books and self-publications. As a matter of fact, among the stacks a few years back was one last copy of this particular writer's first novel. Yes, a very cool place indeed.

Borderline Tap

1958 W. North Avenue 773-278-5138
Hours: Sun–Fri, 1 P.M.–4 A.M.; Sat, 1 P.M.–5 A.M.

I have mixed feelings about Borderline. If you try to go come here after the 2 A.M. bars close, good luck finding a place to stand let alone being able to wade your way up to the bar. During the afternoon, however, Borderline is a sunny, quiet place to kick back and down a few. Of particular merit are the number of windows running the length of the space. Watching people wander about the big six-corner intersection is always an enjoyable endeavor. They have some good beers on tap, too, including BBK, which always seems to make me a bit loopy—not drunk loopy, but disoriented loopy. Sort of the same feeling you get after eating a big chunk of government cheese. Hmm, perhaps there's a connection. . . .

Red Dog

1958 W. North Avenue 773-278-5138
Hours: Mon, 10 P.M.–4 a.m.; Wed, 10 A.M.–4 P.M.;
Fri–Sat, 10 P.M.–4 A.M.

For those who like authentic, sweaty, high-energy dance clubs that aren't full of either suburbanites or yuppies, this is your place. Red Dog has been around for years now. Covers are typically five bucks or less during the week and go up to a stiff ten bucks on Fridays and Saturdays (yes, I realize I'm probably showing my age by blanching at that price). Still, if you're into dancing and despise all those trendy, here-today-gone-tomorrow, hyped-up monstrosities that pop up in warehouses every other week, this is your place.

City Soles

2001 W. North Avenue 773-489-2001
Hours: Mon–Wed, 11 A.M.–8 P.M.; Thu–Fri, 11 A.M.–
9 P.M.; Sat, 11 A.M.–8 P.M.; Sun, 11 A.M.–6 P.M.

The place to buy hipster shoes in Wicker Park. This is a big, bright, comfortable shop with a wide selection for both men and women. Many of these are quite expensive, but they do cut prices drastically for seasonal sales. If you can hit this store right before the change of seasons, you can clean up. Otherwise expect to dish out some dough.

Estelle's

2013 W. North Avenue 773-782-0450
Hours: Mon–Fri, 5 P.M.–4 A.M.; Sat, 7 P.M.–5 A.M.;
Sun, 7 P.M.–4 A.M.

Estelle's—or "It Smells" as many refer to it—is the sort of afterhours bar you never want to go to but occasionally find yourself in anyway. Small and smoky, with a pool table taking up valuable space, Estelle's is full of sleazy shenanigans and drunken ugliness pretty much every night. Yet even though it takes you forever to get the hard-working bartender's attention and the possibility of ever grabbing a stool is nonexistent, there is a certain charm to this place. But try not to go in there in a bad mood because you'll only make it worse. From a sociological perspective Estelle's can be interesting— especially on open mike nights during the week. Just be prepared to find yourself filled with bile and moral grime by the time you leave.

Handlebar

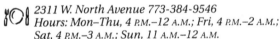

2311 W. North Avenue 773-384-9546
Hours: Mon–Thu, 4 P.M.–12 A.M.; Fri, 4 P.M.–2 A.M.;
Sat, 4 P.M.–3 A.M.; Sun, 11 A.M.–12 A.M.

This establishment is a recent addition to North Avenue, and a welcome one it is. As the name suggests, this place is "bicycle-themed," with quite a bit of the furniture comprised of old bike parts. They also host "Messenger Mondays," when bike messengers can get free plates of fries, and have plenty of free bike parking. Live music is occasionally offered, and the menu offers some very interesting, vegetarian-heavy fare. A unique, friendly little place.

Thai Lagoon

2322 W. North Avenue 773-489-5747
Hours: Mon–Thu, 5 P.M.–10 P.M.; Fri, 5 P.M.–11 P.M.;
Sat, 9 A.M.–3 P.M. and 5 P.M.–11 P.M.; Sun, 9 A.M.–3 P.M.
and 4 P.M.–9:30 P.M.

This attractive, sleekly designed restaurant serves up a
tasty batch of traditional and "experimental" Thai
dishes and features an interesting mix of artwork that
changes frequently. If you like good spicy food to the
accompaniment of ambient tunes, this is definitely a
place to check out.

DAMEN AVENUE

Damen comes squirting up through East Village, and almost
immediately after crossing Chicago Avenue begins hipsteriz-
ing. Though a few ethnic businesses still exist south of
Division, the same cannot be said once you're past the
North/Milwaukee intersection. You are now in the heart of
Bucktown, the most gentrified section of West Town, with
condos and trendy restaurants aplenty, as well as several
pricey women's clothing boutiques. This goes on all the way
to Fullerton.

Lava Lounge

859 N. Damen Avenue 773-772-3355
Hours: Sun–Fri, 5 P.M.–2 A.M.; Sat, 7 P.M.–3 A.M.

Though Lava Lounge definitely attracts a very "stylish"
crowd, with DJ's spinning throughout the week, it's still
a small, low-key, mellow bar to hang out in. From the
dimly lit main area you can ascend a few stairs and
kick back in a handful of rooms. The space was originally an apartment, and it still retains the same
dimensions. Here you'll find couches, a pool table, and
a pinball machine as well. Kicking back in these upper
rooms is sort of akin to hanging out at home, except,
of course, you have to pay for drinks. But let's face it,

the sort of people that hang out here probably wouldn't want to hang out at your place, so it's a pretty good trade-off.

Rainbo Club

1150 N. Damen Avenue 773-489-5999
Hours: Sun–Fri, 4 P.M.–2 A.M.; Sat, 4 P.M.–3 A.M.

Nelson Algren no doubt downed a few in this dark little bar, as it's been around since the days of the Polish ghetto. Rather than catering to working-class stiffs, though, Rainbo has been a meeting place for Wicker Park hipsters for many years now. Wicker Park was still a bit sketchy by the time this conversion took place, and you'll still find a number of old-timer artists about the bar every now and then. I must say Rainbo always seems to bring in a large smattering of nattily dressed art gals—and guys too, I guess. Though I don't go there that often these days, back when I was a young man just out of college and mistakenly engaged to be married, it was a bit of a dangerous place. Dangerous in the sense that practically anywhere I looked there were handfuls of appealing women. Ah youth . . . it is, as they say, wasted on the young.

Pontiac Café

1531 N. Damen Avenue 773-252-7767
Hours: Sun–Fri, 11:30 A.M.–2 A.M.; Sat, 11:30 A.M.–3 A.M.

 This place started out a couple years back as a simple deli serving up vegetarian and low-fat, "healthy" items, but they've since added a bar and a huge outdoor patio for the spring and summer months. A nice place to kick back and eat some food, but don't come here expecting to eat a huge greasy burger. Live music is now offered, as well as occasional poetry readings and such. A great place for people watching.

Artful Dodger

1734 W. Wabansia Avenue 773-227-6859
Hours: Mon–Fri, 5 P.M.–2 A.M.; Sat, 8 P.M.–3 A.M.;
Sun, 8 P.M.–2 A.M.

A Bucktown institution, Artful Dodger is the place to go to dance if you're not into the club scene. Very casual and laid-back—not to mention small, dim, and colorful—this is a comfortable little joint. On Fridays and Saturdays they charge a small cover of $2.

WESTERN AVENUE

Western begins its chug through West Town in Ukrainian Village. You'll find that Western is the least gentrified street in the neighborhood. But for a couple of places in Ukrainian Village, it's the same as it was years ago, with a large number of Mexican-owned used-car dealerships and various groceries and such. This continues all the way to Fullerton and beyond, where the ethnic makeup of the street may change, but not its overall character.

Bar Vertigo

853 N. Western Avenue 773-395-3002
Hours: Open every day, 8 P.M.–2 A.M.

A throwback to the bars of the old Wicker Park, Bar Vertigo is a laid-back, casual joint, Alfred Hitchcock murals notwithstanding. DJs spin throughout the week, while local bands play on weekends. You're not likely to see the second coming of Nirvana here, but you can see Stardust, the David Bowie tribute band. There's also cheap beer available along with the good stuff. What more could you ask for?

Empty Bottle

1035 N. Western Avenue 773-276-3600
Hours: Mon–Wed, 5 P.M.–2 A.M.; Thu-Fri, 3 P.M.–2 A.M.;
Sat, 12 P.M.–3 A.M.; Sun, 12 P.M.–2 A.M.

West Town's premier small venue for local and national acts. Drinks are no longer dirt cheap like they used to be, but this is one of the more laid-back, independent joints in town. Booking at Empty Bottle definitely reflects the attitude and tastes of its owner, and whether or not you get into the hipper-than-thou, art-student rock bands you're most likely to see play here, you have to admire the fact that this bar is run less for profit than as a showcase for music. Live music is offered seven nights a week, along with a jazz show-case on Wednesdays. Bite, the eatery within Empty Bottle, serves up "healthy" fare with a penchant for pasta dishes and vegetarian sandwiches at decent prices. They open at noon every day, and on weekends you can order from the bar at that hour as well.

New World Resource Center

1300 N. Western Avenue 773-227-4011
Hours: Tue–Fri, 3 P.M.–9 P.M.; Sat–Sun, 12 P.M.–7 P.M.

This unique bookshop, here at its newest location, bills itself as Chicago's only "all points of view to the left" bookstore. This is not entirely true as there are a couple of other such stores in the city, but I'll willingly give New World plenty of bragging rights. This is an excellent store, its interior filled with plenty of hard-to-find books concerned with, well, "points of view to the left. " These range from environmental and political treatises to topics such as the women's movement and labor struggles. The bargain table has some of the best 99¢ books you're ever apt to find. They also sell period-icals, CDs, cassettes, T-shirts, and buttons. Well worth checking out.

Margie's Candies

1960 N. Western Avenue 773-384-1035
Hours: Open every day, 9 A.M.–1 A.M.

Back when I use to live in the area, I was always afraid Margie's might fall victim to gentrification and disappear. The place is still going strong, I'm happy to say, as it has been since the '20s. Though they offer regular diner fare, the homemade candies and ice cream are the real draw. For my money, you will not have a better shake or malt—or sundae or banana split, for that matter—anywhere in the city. This place is a national treasure.

Arturo's

2001 N. Western Avenue 773-772-4944
Hours: Open 24 hours

Though Lazo's next door is much bigger and less crowded, this tiny taqueria serves up better grub. This place is justifiably packed during the wee hours. Might I suggest the torta milenasa?

The Gallery Cabaret

2020 N. Oakley Avenue 773-489-5471
Hours: Sun–Fri, 5 P.M.–2 a.m.; Sat, 5 P.M.–3 A.M.

Ah, Gallery Cabaret. What can one say about such a place? Well, I suppose one could call it a blue-collar hipster bar. Maybe. Actually, there's no way to describe the damn place that would do it justice. With decor straight out of your lascivious Uncle Louie's basement circa 1970 and a collection of oddballs—lovable and otherwise—as its patrons, Gallery Cabaret is an interesting place to visit. And you should try to visit when a band is playing so that you can watch the transformation of the owner as he tends bar. This man is a nice, low-key individual, but as the place becomes a bit crowded, his movements grow disturbingly frantic as he rushes about to service his patrons. But not frantic in a chicken-with-its-head-cut-off way, but rather in a robotic, herky-jerky manner, as if someone just flipped a switch on the back of his neck. It's quite a sight. So yes, this place belongs on your itinerary if for no other reason than that.

Quenchers

2401 N. Western Avenue 773-276-9730
Hours: Sun–Fri, 11 A.M.–2 A.M.; Sat, 11 A.M.–3 A.M.

Quenchers has been around for almost twenty-five years and draws a truly mixed, genial crowd. This is definitely the place to go for you beer connoisseurs, for they actually have two hundred different bottled beers, along with eighteen on tap. Their lunch menu is also one of the best values in town, with chili, bratwurst, and other sandwiches starting at $2. As if this isn't enough, they also feature free live acts six nights a week, with an "indie rock" open mike on Mondays. The acts are quite varied as well, ranging in style from your typical indie rock to jazz and Afro-Cuban pop. One of the best bars in the city.

The Mutiny

2428 N. Western Avenue 773-486-7774
Hours: Sun–Fri, 11 A.M.–2 A.M.; Sat, 7 A.M.–3 A.M.

The Mutiny is not one of the best bars in the city. But that's okay, because it certainly isn't trying to be. Here in this nondescript tavern you can drink nondescript beer, listen to tunes on the nondescript jukebox and play nondescript pool. You can also catch nondescript bands, and therein lies the charm. Anyone can play here. Just formed a band a week ago? Give them a call. The bands are your typical indie rock and punk outfits, whose attributes vary widely. As such joints fade into oblivion in the Wicker Park/Bucktown area, places like The Mutiny become ever more important, whether they put much energy into the effort or not.

7

HUMBOLDT PARK

Named for the expansive park at its heart, Humboldt Park is heavily Hispanic. The city's Puerto Rican population is centered here, and many African Americans also reside in the neighborhood. Though plenty of comfortable, working-class families live here, there is also quite a bit of poverty in certain areas, and for many years some of the commercial streets looked like deserted wastelands. Needless to say, rising prices in Wicker Park has created plenty of spillover, as many young "artistes" have been forced to move to Humboldt Park—or, as some Realtors call it—"West Wicker Park." This appellation isn't entirely inaccurate, as Humboldt Park's eastern border is essentially California Avenue, but there is still a different atmosphere once you cross Western Avenue. That's why I've lumped the following businesses together under Humboldt Park, even though a couple of them are indeed in "West Wicker Park." Plenty of Realtors, however, use the West Wicker Park label for residences well past California Avenue, hence the snicker most Chicagoans will let loose when they hear the phrase. Whatever the case, gentrification—though it probably will come eventually—does not yet appear to be any seri-

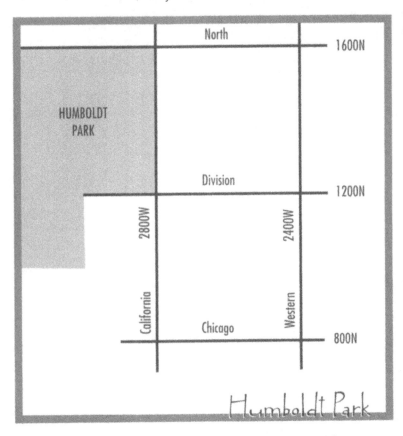

North

1600N

HUMBOLDT
PARK

Division

1200N

2800W

2400W

California

Western

Chicago

800N

Humboldt Park

ous threat beyond the area immediately west of Western Avenue. As of now, there are just a few places to hit, but if you're looking for a photo op, you can't do much better than snapping a few shots under the gigantic Puerto Rican flag arch that spans Division Street just past Western.

Tommy's Rock 'n' Roll Café

2500 W. Chicago Avenue 773-486-6768
Hours: Mon–Fri, 7:30 A.M.–6 P.M.; Sat, 7:30 A.M.–3:30 P.M.;
Sun, 7:30 A.M.–3 P.M.

One of the more unique businesses in the city, Tommy's offers both food and guitars— not to mention records, wrestling figures, and fishing lures, among other things. Musicians may be more excited by all the instruments and amps, but I particularly covet the sloppy joes on the menu. Alongside the traditional burgers and dogs also offered, the sloppy joe definitely reigns supreme. I know they're not hard to make at home, but somehow Tommy's just does them up right.

Black Beetle Bar & Grill

2532 W. Chicago Avenue 773-384-0701
Hours: Sun–Fri, 5 P.M.–2 A.M.; Sat, 5 P.M.–3 A.M.

The Black Beetle has been around for a few years now and is definitely prospering. This large joint, with an atypical layout, is a convivial place to down some beer and food. The jukebox is excellent, and you'll find the atmosphere very down-to-earth. What you get here is a Wicker Park–type bar without the attitude.

Flying Saucer

1123 N. California Avenue 773-342-9076
Hours: Tue–Fri, 7 A.M.–10 P.M.; Sat, 8 A.M.–10 P.M.;
Sun, 8 A.M.–3 P.M.

This attractive, laid-back, interesting restaurant has something for everyone. From typical diner fare like meatloaf to fancy dinner specials, from Belgian waffles to breakfast burritos, from meat-heavy to vegan. It is as if the owner did indeed arrive in a flying saucer and, having only a rudimentary knowledge of the human restaurant industry, decided to go for broke and appeal to as many earthlings as possible. The experiment has indeed been successful, with the entrées ranging from very good to outright amazing. Hell, they even have a pastry chef. And I haven't even mentioned that it's BYOB! If you're in the area, don't miss it.

The California Clipper Lounge

1002 N. California Avenue 773-384-2547
Hours: Sun–Fri, 8 P.M.–2 A.M.; Sat, 8 P.M.–3 A.M.

What was a neighborhood "old man" bar only a few years ago has been transformed into a very attractive, '40s-esque lounge. In its earlier days you could consider it a jazz club, but now the music acts that play here on weekends range in style from country to blues. Though there's never a cover for bands, this is not a cheap place to drink, something that may throw you considering its "out-of-the-way" location. It certainly did me. On my first visit here I had to unexpectedly whip out the credit card to buy a reciprocal round. If, however, you don't mind spending the money and would like to sip a martini or beer in a very well-done retro setting, this is your place.

Lilly's Record Shop

2733 W. Division Street 773-252-7008
Hours: Mon–Sat, 11 A.M.–9 P.M.; Sun, 11 A.M.–7:30 P.M.

This little shop has been around for twenty years, offering up a wide variety of Latin music, from salsa and merengue to many other styles I'm much too white and untutored to tell apart.

La Bruquena

2726 W. Division Street 773-276-2915
Hours: Open every day, 9 A.M.–11:30 P.M.

Serving up the best Puerto Rican fare in the city, this upscale restaurant offers a variety of dishes, the best of which, in my opinion, is their specialty, the mashed green plantain with fried pork. Plenty of tropical drinks and desserts await you as well, and every Friday a live Latin jazz band plays in the second floor lounge. La Bruquena isn't cheap, but if you're in the mood for Puerto Rican food or have never tried it, this is a great place to visit.

8
LOGAN SQUARE

Logan Square had its heyday in the 1890s. Well-off merchants of various white ethnicities—Germans, Poles, Norwegians—built some very imposing homes along Logan Boulevard. Most of them are still standing today and function as apartment buildings. And let me tell you, these apartments are huge. I've been to a few parties in Logan Square, and I must say the apartments are among some of the nicest I've ever seen. According to my mother, who grew up in the city, Logan Square was still considered a nice neighborhood through the '40s and into the '50s. That soon changed. By the early '60s the neighborhood had fallen into neglect, and Puerto Rican immigrants began moving in to take advantage of the cheap rents. Logan Square to this day remains heavily Puerto Rican. There was some trouble with gangs in the '80s and early '90s, but for the most part—unlike Humboldt Park—the neighborhood has developed into a desirable place to live. Despite the number of youthful whites who have begun moving in, the area has retained its Latin flavor, with scores of Puerto Rican kids "cruisin'" the boulevard on weekends.

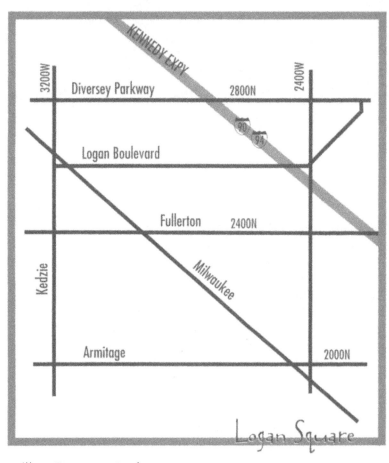

Village Discount Outlet

2032 N. Milwaukee Avenue
Hours: Mon–Fri, 9 A.M.–9 P.M.; Sat, 9 A.M.–6 P.M.;
Sun, 11 A.M.–5 P.M.

This is my all-time favorite Village Discount. Sure its two floors are crowded and cluttered, but you can always find a decent selection of jeans and slacks that—if good for nothing else—can be cut into shorts. There's also plenty of shirts and women's clothing, books, albums, and coats. The few good items take some finding among the less savory ones, but it's always worth the search.

Blue Willow

 2418 W. Fullerton Avenue 773-384-6499
Hours: Open every day, 11 A.M.–10 P.M.

A small, no-frills Chinese restaurant, Blue Willow has
been transplanted from its former digs at Chicago and
Damen Avenue. I wouldn't say the food is particularly
outstanding, but it's good, decent fare at cheap prices.
Back when it was still in East Village, Blue Willow stood
out for the simple fact that it was a no-frills joint, as
opposed to the more expensive, upscale Asian restaurants that began popping up. There aren't too many
other little Chinese joints in the area, so if you're in the
neighborhood and have a sudden hankering for some
fried rice, give it a visit.

Fireside Bowl

2646 W. Fullerton Avenue 773-486-2700
Hours: Varies depending on show, but generally open
every day from 7 P.M.–1 A.M.

Strangely enough, this small old bowling alley has
become an all-ages punk rock mecca featuring bands
every night. On its small stage you can see anyone
from known national acts to local suburban outfits
playing their first gig—the members barely having
mastered puberty let alone their instruments. Not long
ago the Fireside's ceiling was collapsing, the bathrooms stunk to high heaven, and the sound was
absolutely terrible—yet you could still bowl at one end
of the joint while bands played at the other. After the
ceiling was shored up, the bathrooms redone, and a
new sound system put in place, you could no longer
bowl. Now that the city has bought the property for a
proposed park extension and Fireside's demise is supposedly imminent, bowling is back, though only on
Monday nights. Go figure. One thing that hasn't
changed is the enclosed bar in the corner, where you
can escape the noise and underage kiddies (believe
me, this is sometimes very necessary). The prices have

gone up and the bartender is more likely to be shooting pool than diligently pouring suds, but so what? In only a few short years this place became a Chicago institution, the likes of which will be hard to replace. And though rumors of its impending doom have been floating about for years, it appears to be about as hard to get rid of as teenage pimples. Before you know it they might even clean the tap lines.

El Nandu

*2731 W. Fullerton Avenue 773-278-0900
Hours: Mon–Wed, 12 P.M.–10:30 P.M.; Thu–Sat,
12 P.M.–2 A.M.; Sun, 4:30 P.M.–10:30 P.M.*

Though I've only eaten at this small, upscale South American restaurant once, I must say I was very impressed by the empanadas. We made a meal of them alone, trying each variety, of which I believe there were about eight. Very, very good—especially the shrimp and cheese one, which I was rather skeptical about before trying it. They also serve up plenty of entrées and make their own sangría. You're going to spend some money here, but if you've got a long night ahead at the Fireside and don't feel like hitting one of the many fast-food options in the vicinity, you can't do much better than El Nandu. If you're around on the weekend you can catch live music on Friday and Saturday night, though I must say the slides of the llamas and other South American sights they project up front is enough entertainment for me in themselves.

9

CLYBOURN CORRIDOR

Clybourn is a diagonal street running northwest through the city from Division on the south to Western on the north. However, it is generally only from Halsted on the south to Fullerton on the north that is referred to as the "Clybourn Corridor." This area was strictly a fading industrial strip all the way up into the '80s. Even as late as '85, what remained outside of the few operating factories was practically a wasteland. This is hardly the case now. Since the late '80s the area has completely turned around, sporting many a monolithic "superstore" such as Home Depot, Sports Authority, and Crate and Barrel. You'll also find plenty of upscale strip malls, expensive restaurants, and boutiques.

Salvation Army Thrift Store

2270 N. Clybourn Avenue 773-477-1771
Hours: Mon–Sat, 10 A.M.–6 P.M.

With its huge parking lot, this is one of the most convenient Salvation Army stores in the city. It's also one of the biggest, with two levels. You're not likely to find too many treasures, but there's a plentiful selection of serviceable clothes and furniture.

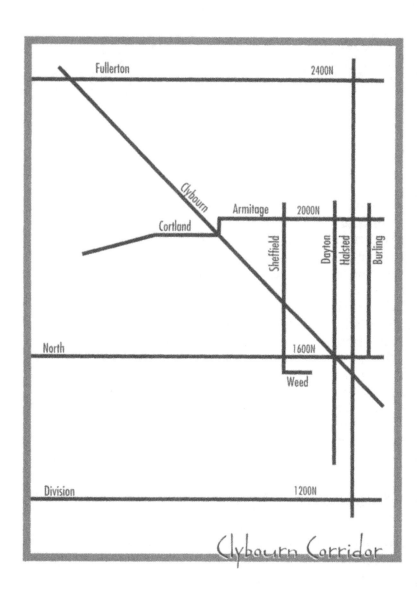

Clybourn Corridor

Liar's Club

1665 W. Fullerton Avenue 773-665-1110
Hours: Sun-Fri, 8 P.M.–2 A.M.; Sat, 8 P.M.–3 A.M.

This dark little club succeeds at being both a cozy place in which to chill out and knock back a few during the off-hours and a place to get nutty on the dance floor amid the heavy crowds during the wee hours. The beer selection is extensive, plenty of quality specials are offered, and DJs spin throughout the week. Upstairs you'll even find a small room with a couple of couches and a pool table—as well as its very own bar. This is a club for people who don't particularly like clubs. The clientele is very down-to-earth and attitude is nonexistent. You also have to admire the ad they used to run some years back in which they would claim to be Chicago's premier ballroom dancing venue, or the city's finest S&M club. Lies all!

Weeds

1555 N. Dayton Street 312-943-7815
Hours: Mon–Sat, 4 P.M.–2 A.M.

A Chicago institution, Weeds has occupied its small chunk of real estate for many a long year now. One of the more offbeat taverns in the city, Weeds is run by an enigmatic man known as Sergio Mayora. The first thing you notice upon entering is a statue of him on the bar. The crowd is laid-back and highly diverse—from senior citizens to young hipsters. Bands jam on the small stage on weekends and the beer garden is one of the best places to be on summer nights. A very original little suds joint.

Sam's Wine and Liquors

1720 N. Marcey Street 312-664-4394
Hours: Mon–Sat, 8 A.M.–9 P.M.; Sun, 11 A.M.–6 P.M.

Sam's has been in the neighborhood for quite some time. It used to be you could browse through its amazing stock of domestic and imported wines, beers, and liquors, then step outside to the solicitations of prostitutes on North Avenue. The prostitutes are gone now, but Sam's—in a new building about a block away—still carries one of the best selections of alcohol in the city. Entering this place gets me keyed up just like toystores used to when I was a kid. Much like Buck, the sled dog hero of *The Call of the Wild*, I fall into a trance, thinking about the good beers I've drunk in the past and the good beers I'd like to drink in the future.

Crobar

1543 N. Kingsbury Street 312-413-7000
Hours: Wed–Fri, 9 P.M.–4 A.M.; Sat, 9 P.M.–5 A.M.;
Sun, 9 P.M.–4 A.M.

Now that I'm an old man, it's been a long time since I've wiggled my butt on the dance floor of a "cutting-edge" nightclub. If the need were ever to arise again, Crobar, which has been around for many years, would be my place of choice. The decor is very industrial and dark and the crowd is a little bit scruffier around the edges than your usual club crowd. Expect to fork over plenty of dough, but if you're into industrial music in particular, you should check this place out.

Exit

1315 W. North Avenue 773-395-2700
Hours: Open every day, 9 P.M.–4 A.M.

This is the same legendary institution that used to call Old Town its home. The Exit of old was always an interesting place. The music strayed toward goth and punk and the crowd ran the gamut from mohawk-sporting youths to suit-and-tie-wearing yuppies. That eclecticism is lost in this new location—and gone are the "penny drink" nights (which, after a bit of reflection, I must proclaim a good thing)—but if you're looking for a dark club in which to drink or get down, this is a grungier alternative to Crobar.

The Hideout

1354 W. Wabansia Avenue 773-227-4433
Hours: Mon, 8 P.M.–2 A.M.; Tue–Fri, 4 P.M.–2 A.M.;
Sat, 7 P.M.–3 A.M.; Sun, varies depending upon event.

Aptly named considering it's very hard to find, the Hideout changed from an old man bar to a music venue a few years back and has truly become (yes, I know I make this claim quite a bit—but it's true!) a Chicago institution. The music takes place nightly in a separate room in back, where acts range from rock to bluegrass with plenty of variations in between, though they do tend to be more "twangy" rather than not. The place can get very crowded sometimes, but you can spill outdoors during the warmer months. The atmosphere is always convivial and upbeat, absolutely free of attitude. The Hideout is indeed one of the best joints in the city.

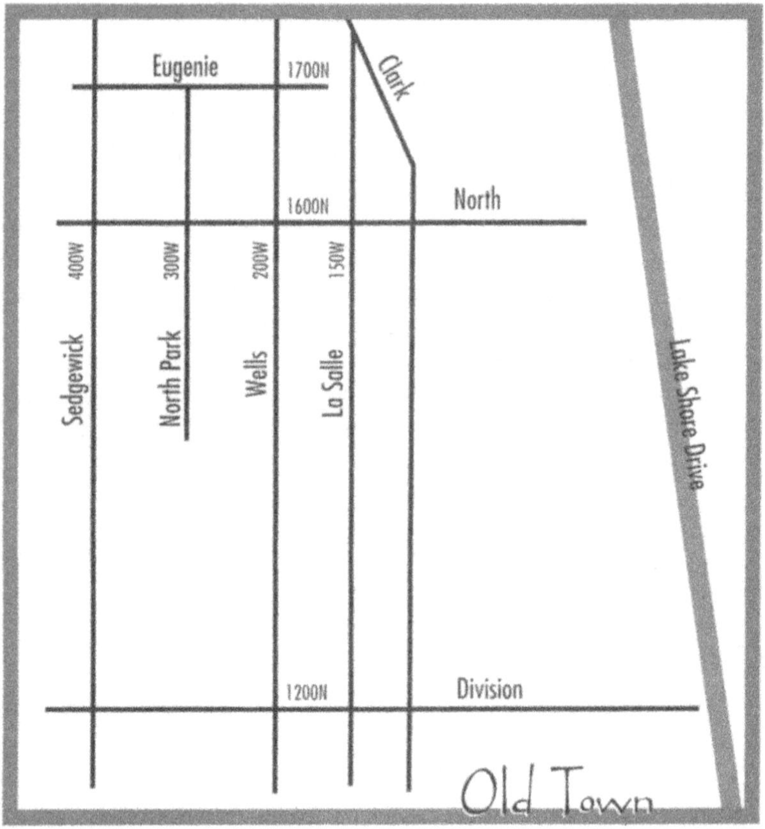
Eugenie
1700N
Clark
1600N
North
400W
300W
200W
150W
Sedgewick
North Park
Wells
La Salle
Lake Shore Drive
1200N
Division
Old Town

10

OLD TOWN

Germans were the first to move here in the 1850s to escape overcrowding in their old neighborhoods, and since then Old Town has played host to Hungarians and even some Italians over the years. Now it's safe to say the only real ethnic group is upper-middle-class, white American. Old Town is a very expensive place to live. Here reside mature, professional families who have left their carefree days of yuppiedom behind. The shops are mostly expensive boutiques, and the restaurants are pricey. Not many vestiges of Old Town's '60s history remain. Back then it was a funky, artsy, "up-and-coming" neighborhood (shades of West Town), but about all that remains of those days are a couple of porno shops. It was here during the '68 Democratic Convention that many hippies and war protesters got their heads bashed in by the cops after nearby Lincoln Park was cleared for the night. The cops weren't satisfied with just the hippies though. They also burst into a few homes, the inhabitants of which were supposedly "taunting" the sensitive souls from their windows. Needless to say, it was "billyclubs-a-go-go" all night long.

Over 21 Bookstore

1347 N. Wells Street 312-337-8730
Hours: Open 24 hours

 As you can no doubt guess from the name, this is an adult bookstore. Not particularly seedy, this is the type of place some of the tipsy, well-heeled patrons of the expensive restaurants nearby might not feel averse to enter on a lark. A typical, unspectacular selection of mags and videos is available for your perusing pleasure.

Bijou Theater

 1349 N. Wells Street 312-943-5397
Hours: Open 24 hours

A Chicago institution, the Bijou has been showing gay porno films for many years now. If you're expecting some sort of seedy joint you'll be disappointed—the Bijou is actually kind of upscale. You're not going to find a motley collection of ne'er-do-wells clandestinely stroking themselves in the dark. That's not to say, however, that there's no stroking going on. . . .

Barbara's Bookstore

1350 N. Wells Street 312-642-5044
Hours: Mon–Sat, 10 A.M.–10 P.M.; Sun, 11 A.M.–8 P.M.

The flagship store of this small Chicago chain, Barbara's is one of the best of the independent shops featuring new books. They carry a great collection of fiction, as well as a very good selection of history, current events, and travel. Outside of the fiction section, you won't find a huge amount of books on any particular subject, but plenty of quality ones.

Adult Books

1405 N. Wells Street
Hours: Open 24 hours

 This small, cramped shop is a typically seedy porno
 joint. In addition to video booths, you'll find many

dog-eared magazines and a selection of videos—both straight and gay. This along with a small amount of "novelties" behind the counter. One of the more interesting aspects of the place is that thrown willy-nilly under one of the bins are several old books—naughty books, you would imagine, but no, among several nondescript titles are books about Karl Marx, Saul Alinksy, and the benefits of socialism.

Up Down Tobacco Shop

1550 N. Wells Street 312-337-8025
Hours: Sun–Thu, 10 A.M.–11 P.M.; Fri–Sat, 10 A.M.–12 A.M.

This spacious, attractive store is a smoking aficionado's dream, filled to the brim with cigars, pipes, humidors, and other such odds and ends, staffed by very knowledgeable, friendly folks. To further propagate the joy of gourmet smoking, the store even sponsors an annual pipe-smoking contest.

Second City Theatre

1616 N. Wells Street 312-337-3992
Hours: Shows are performed throughout the week; call for specifics.

A renowned Chicago institution, the Second City Theatre specializes in improv comedy. Take any past, current, or future *Saturday Night Live* cast and chances are at least half of them will be Second City alumni, from the Belushis to Chris Farley.

See Hear Inc.

217 W. North Avenue 312-664-6285
Hours: Mon–Sat, 10 A.M.–9 P.M.; Sun 10 A.M.–6 P.M.

This record shop stocks a decent selection of new and used CDs. The international section is particularly strong, though all sections are well-stocked, not just the pop/rock bins.

Old Town Ale House

219 W. North Avenue 312-944-7020
Hours: Sun–Fri, 12 P.M.–4 A.M.; Sat, 12 P.M.–5 A.M.

This old tavern is a bit of a Chicago institution. Within its confines you'll find plenty of social drinkers rubbing shoulders with serious barflies—quite a number of them upscale sorts with decent careers . . . at least for now. Though nothing special, Old Town Ale House is a laid-back, low-key joint in which to get wasted. The key word here being *wasted*—not an activity that is generally smiled upon in most of the bars in this part of the city. Sure they'll take your money and get you wasted, but once you've achieved that goal you can pretty well bet they'll be showing you the door the second you start slurring. At Old Town you can slur as much as you want to.

11

LINCOLN PARK

Before the Great Fire, Lincoln Park alongside the lake was a cemetery. After the fire, the graves were removed further north and the area was turned into a park. Many German families began buying lots and building houses to the west of the park, while wealthy Anglos bought up the expensive properties immediately fronting the park. This property facing the park remains very expensive and desirable to this day, and the area immediately to the west—though it had its problems up into the '60s—now enjoys the same status. In fact, by the '80s Lincoln Park was the premier stomping ground of Chicago's yuppies. Most of these original yuppies have grown older and procreated, giving Lincoln Park—at least along Clark Street—a less festive atmosphere these days. But along Lincoln Avenue there are yuppie night spots aplenty. In fact, all of Lincoln Park is full of expensive eateries, pubs, and boutiques, but it is Lincoln Avenue between Fullerton and Sheffield that is the hot spot for partying, especially since Depaul University is in the vicinity. There are plenty of shops for every taste in the neighborhood, not to mention scads of coffee shops and bakeries and such. And if the shopping and eat-

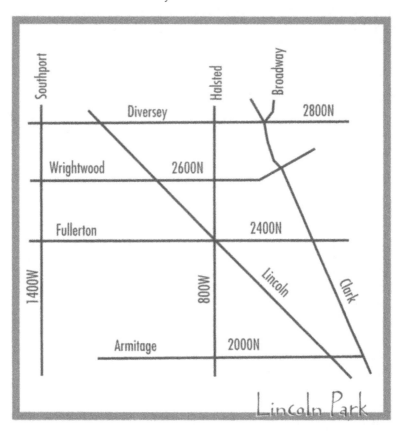

ing begin to lose their luster, the park and lake are but a short walk away. Lincoln Park Zoo sets up shop here too—and admission is free.

Big John's Joint

1147 W. Armitage Avenue 773-477-4400
Hours: Sun–Fri, 11 A.M.–2 P.M.; Sat, 11 A.M.–3 P.M.

This is a low-key sports bar with a mostly middle-aged crowd. What sets it apart is its food. Burgers are their specialty, but the homemade chili is quite good as well. It's also one of the few places in the city where you can get a liverwurst sandwich. I briefly worked here several years ago, and I can attest to the fact that the owner orders only the finest ingredients. And now that I'm no longer bumbling ineptly about the grill, the food's probably even better. A nice place to visit in both winter and summer, as you can either take advantage of the beer garden out back or the fireplace in the main room.

Neo

2350 N. Clark Street 773-528-2622
Hours: Sun–Fri, 10 A.M.–4 P.M.; Sat, 10 A.M.–5 P.M.

A Chicago institution, Neo has been serving the "alternative" dance crowd for about twenty years now. They host various theme nights during the week, and you'll find their "goth" night is one of the more popular. And I must confess— though I once was goth myself—it's always rather amusing to see people getting down dramatically to the bouncy, irresistible beat of "Bela Lugosi's Dead." (For you non-goths, I'm being very sarcastic about that particular song's danceability. Imagine dancing to a Gregorian Chant and you'll get the idea.)

Amigos & Us

2443 N. Clark Street 773-529-6476
Hours: Mon–Sat, 12 P.M.–8 P.M.; Sun, 1 P.M.–6 P.M.

This friendly shop proudly bills itself as a "full-service" hippie boutique and gift shop. Here you'll find scads of tie-dyed and hippie-esque clothing, as well as jewelry and accessories. They also carry plenty of incense and rolling papers. For you Deadheads out there, this is a must-visit, while even the most strident right-wingers won't be able to resist a genuine smile or two upon entering. This place could mellow out even Sean Hannity from the Fox Misinformation Channel (oops, I mean News Channel).

Hi-Fi Records

2570 N. Clark Street 773-880-1002
Hours: Mon–Sat, 11 A.M.–8 P.M.; Sun, 12 P.M.–7 P.M.

 Hi-Fi sports an impressive selection of new, used, and rare LPs, 12"s, and 45s. From lounge crooners of old to just-released Jamaican dancehall, this shop has a bit of everything. Originally they dealt exclusively with vinyl, but they now also carry plenty of CDs, videos, and DVDs.

Graham Crackers Comics

2562 N. Clark Street 773-665-2010
Hours: Mon–Sat, 11 A.M.–7 P.M.; Sun, 12 P.M.–5 P.M.

Much larger than the Loop store, this location has thousands of comics, with an outstanding collection of new titles and back issues, both from independents and big boys like Marvel and DC. In addition you'll find the usual toys and T-shirts and such.

Boxcar Cafe

728 W. Wrightwood 773-325-9560
Hours: Mon–Fri, 7 A.M.–9 P.M.; Sat–Sun, 10 A.M.–9 P.M.

Feeling jaded and at odds with the world? Well, this is the place for you. The Boxcar Cafe could provoke a genuine smile even in a man like Dick Cheney. In this small, homey little coffee shop you can have your drinks and ice cream delivered by train. Yes, train. Toy trains, of course, but trains nonetheless. There are also plenty of games for both kids and adults, as well as chalk, with which you can write on the floor and walls. Sure, it's a bit gimmicky, I suppose, but so what—the place is fun. And let's not forget the coffee and grub, which is the reason you're supposed to come here in the first place. What you'll find is good solid fare, from the coffee and smoothies to the pastries, ice cream, sandwiches, and salads. But let's face it, it's the trains that are really going to bring you in. *Whoa nelly!*

Dave's Records

🎵 *2604 N. Clark Street 773-929-6325*
Hours: Mon–Sat, 11 A.M.–8 P.M.; Sun, 12 P.M.–7 P.M.

Occupying what used to be a 2nd Hand Tunes "annex," Dave's is the place to go for vinyl nuts. As they proudly proclaim, "CDs—never had 'em, never will." The variety here is incredible, from rock and newer "drum and bass" stuff to old, rare comedy albums. You could easily spend a day here browsing. Of course if you do so it would probably be rude if you didn't buy something, but that's not a problem, for I can't imagine anyone not being able to find at least a few albums they would have to take home with them. Hell, my turntable barely works anymore, and I still find myself popping in here every now and then buying stuff I can only rarely listen to. No vinyl aficionado's trip to Chicago would be complete without a stop here.

2nd Hand Tunes

🎵 *2602 N. Clark Street 773-281-8813*
Hours: Mon–Sat, 10 P.M.–10 P.M.; Sun, 10 P.M.–8 P.M.

 One of Chicago's best used record stores, 2nd Hand Tunes has been a Clark Street mainstay for a long time. Here you can find a wide variety of vinyl—from rock and jazz to folk and comedy—along with CDs, cassettes, videos, and DVDs. They even have a few laser discs in addition to a large array of posters in back.

Gramaphone Ltd.

🎵 *2663 N. Clark Street 773-472-3683*
Hours: Mon–Fri, 11 P.M.–9 P.M.; Sat, 10:30 P.M.–8:30 P.M.;
Sun, 11 P.M.–7 P.M.

Chicago's premier record shop for modern dance music. Though you'll find a number of CDs, Gramaphone primarily carries vinyl for DJs. House, techno, ambient—you'll find the best selection in the city here. You can also find plenty of mixes from local DJs.

Untitled

2705 N. Clark Street 773-404-9225
Hours: Mon–Fri, 11 P.M.–8 P.M.; Sat, 10 P.M.–7 P.M.;
Sun, 12 P.M.–7 P.M.

Clothing for the youthful hipster. Though the prices aren't cheap, you can find a large collection of new shirts, tanks, and jeans here. A good deal of it is definitely geared toward the younger crowd, but there's enough variety of stock here to appeal to a pretty wide range of tastes.

Duke of Perth

2913 N. Clark Street 773-477-1741
Hours: Tue–Fri, 11:30 P.M.–2 P.M.; Sat, 11:30 P.M.–3 P.M.;
Sun, 12 P.M.–2 P.M.

This attractive, cozy bar is owned by a real live Scotsman and features a great selection of beer, ale, cider, and scotch. The kitchen turns out tasty treats like Shepherd's pie, and every Wednesday and Friday you can stuff yourself silly with all-you-can-eat fish-frys. These events are not for the claustrophobic, however, as they tend to get quite crowded. Patience is a required virtue as well.

Bookman's Corner

2959 N. Clark Street 773-929-8298
Hours: Mon–Sat, 12 P.M.–8 P.M.; Sun, 12 P.M.–6 P.M.

Bookman's Corner has been in the used-book business forever. Small and cramped with its books piled willy-nilly on the shelves, it's not the most convenient place to search for a particular title. Yet a general browse through the dusty stacks always manages to turn up plenty of interesting stuff.

Facets Multimedia Center

1517 W. Fullerton Avenue 773-281-4114
Hours: Call or check paper for screenings; video rental
Mon–Sat, 10 A.M.–10 P.M.; Sun, 12 P.M.–10 P.M.

Combination cinema, video rental outlet, and resource center, Facets' small theater features a varied line-up of independent and foreign films throughout the week. Their video rental selection is by far the best in the city. You name it, they have it—except for maybe twenty copies of *Gigli* or *The Fast and the Furious*.

BW-3 Grill & Bar

2464 N. Lincoln Avenue 773-868-9453
Hours: Mon, 11 A.M.–12 P.M.; Tue–Fri, 11 A.M.–2 P.M.;
Sat, 11 A.M.–3 P.M.; Sun, 11 A.M.–1 P.M.

BW-3 is part of a large chain, but don't let that scare you off—they cook up the best damn wings in the city. A large bar/restaurant catering to the post-collegiate set, the place can get a bit loud during games, but they do have a take-out window in back so you can avoid that scene if you wish. In addition to the wings, they serve up some tasty bar food—from burgers to Mexican concoctions. They also feature daily lunch specials, along with 30¢ wings on Tuesdays.

Act I Bookstore

2221 N. Lincoln Avenue 773-348-6757
Hours: Mon–Wed, 10 A.M.–8 P.M.; Thu–Sun, 10 A.M.–6 P.M.

This shop specializes in drama. You'll find slews of plays as well as screenplays, lyrics from Broadway musicals, and books on acting and directing. Also, the store encourages local playwrights to drop off scripts, which customers can read in the store.

Kingston Mines

2548 N. Halsted Street 773-477-4646
Hours: Sun–Fri, 8 P.M.–4 A.M.; Sat, 8 P.M.–5 A.M.

Though this legendary club is big enough to sport two stages, the atmosphere remains very intimate—as well as loud, dark, and smoky: the perfect environment in which to see a blues band. Many famous folk have also thought so, from the Rolling Stones and the Who to Michael Jordan and various Hollywood types. The kitchen is open nightly and serves up ribs, hot wings, and catfish. Combine the latter with some good beer and blues, and you got yourself a good night out. Just be sure to bring plenty of cash.

The Prodigal Son

2626 N. Halsted Street 773-248-3093
Hours: Mon–Fri, 5 P.M.–2 A.M.; Sat, 3 P.M.–3 A.M.;
Sun, 3 P.M.–2 A.M.

This neighborhood hasn't seen the likes of the Prodigal Son in years, at least not since the late, great Lounge Ax closed its doors. While not exactly up to the level of Lounge Ax, the Prodigal Son is a comfortable, almost rustic little bar featuring raucous indie rock bands six nights a week, with a jazz open mike night on Wednesdays. The bands play in a small room away from the main bar, so you can sample the excellent beer selection in relative quiet should you choose to do so. In the main bar you can also peruse the extensive "gourmet" grilled cheese menu, with plenty of entries to please both carnivores and vegetarians. This place would be welcome in any neighborhood, but it is a definite breath of fresh (or would that be fetid) air in Lincoln Park.

Village Discount Outlet

2855 N. Halsted Street
Hours: Mon–Fri, 9 A.M.–9 P.M.; Sat, 9 A.M.–6 P.M.;
Sun, 11 A.M.–5 P.M.

This location is much smaller than most of the Village Discounts but does manage to remain consistent with the others in the fact that its prices are cheap, its aisles are crowded, its interior is hot and mildly stinky, and its merchandise has been picked over innumerable times. But then again, you never know. You might get lucky.

Mount Sinai Hospital Resale Shop

814 W. Diversey Parkway 773-935-1434
Hours: Mon–Wed, 10 A.M.–4 P.M.; Thu, 10 A.M.–7 P.M.;
Fri, 10 A.M.–4 P.M.; Sat, 9 A.M.–4 P.M.; Sun, 12 P.M.–4:30 P.M.

This is sort of the Marshall Field's of resale shops. In this well-organized store you'll find plenty of high-quality merchandise. It's going to cost you, but it is, of course, for a good cause.

12

LAKEVIEW

The village of Lakeview in the mid-1800s was not much more than a smattering of farms and summer homes. There was plenty of room to spread out and breathe. This proved an attractive lure for the German families who lived in the congested neighborhood of Old Town in the 1880s. Other ethnic groups—primarily Swedes—followed their lead, and by 1920 Lakeview had close to 100,000 residents. Lakeview is still a very attractive place to live, and for many years was home to a mainly white, working-class population, with a sizable Mexican presence as well. Over the last decade numerous white-collar professionals (and Billy Corgan of Smashing Pumpkins) either began renting in the neighborhood or buying houses, driving up rents and property taxes so that only remnants of the older population remains. This is hardly surprising when you consider that within Lakeview's environs are some of the city's most popular neighborhoods like New Town (or Boys Town as it's informally known) and Wrigleyville. Lakeview covers a lot of territory, and there are plenty of "sub-neighborhoods" within its boundaries. These areas will be treated separately. In addition to the aforemen-

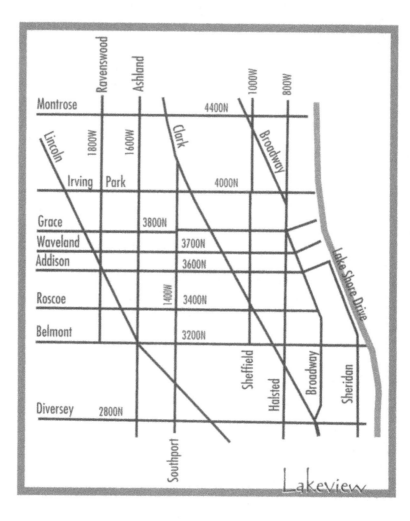

tioned Boys Town and Wrigleyville, these include the Belmont/Clark area, Southport Avenue, St. Ben's, Ravenswood, Roscoe Village, and Lincoln Square. Businesses that don't easily fit into one of these "sub-hoods" are listed here.

Delilah's

2771 N. Lincoln Avenue 773-472-2771
Hours: Sun–Fri, 4 P.M.–2 A.M.; Sat, 4 P.M.–3 A.M.

Old punk rockers never die, they just go to Delilah's.
You won't find a high volume of yuppies here like
most area bars. Delilah's caters instead to seasoned
veterans of Chicago's "underground" scene. Many of
the DJs who spin nightly are from legendary (or at
least semi-legendary) Chicago bands, and the atmosphere is laid-back yet festive. They also have an
incredible selection of beer, as well as more kinds of
whiskey than you ever imagined existed. Early in the
evening on weekends they even host screenings of old
campy horror films, such as *Fatal Flying Guillotines*
and *Kingdom of the Spiders*. This in addition to plenty
of drink specials. This place is definitely worth your
while to visit.

Powell's Bookstore

2850 N. Lincoln Avenue 773-248-1444
Hours: Sun–Fri, 11 A.M.–9 P.M.; Sat, 10 A.M.–10 P.M.

One of three Powell's in Chicago, this one—as always—
upholds the high Powell's standards you'll find in each
of their locations. Large and spacious, this store carries
a great, quality selection of used books on every subject. They even have a rare book room as well as bargain tables. One of the North Side's best shops.

Muskies

2870 N. Lincoln Avenue 773-883-1633
Hours: Mon–Sat, 11 A.M.–10 P.M.

Muskies is a classic burger joint serving up typical fast
food, from burgers and hot dogs to charbroiled
chicken sandwiches. Prices are cheap and the French
fries are not only tasty but very liberally doled out.
Though there is only a small counter and a handful of
stools, in the summer they have a few tables set up

outside. A good place to dart into between bands at the Elbo Room.

Elbo Room

 2871 N. Lincoln Avenue 773-549-5549
Hours: Sun–Fri, 7 P.M.–2 A.M.; Sat, 7 P.M.–3 A.M.

 One of Chicago's more intimate clubs in which to see local bands, Elbo Room is also one of the more attractive ones as well. The upper floor is your typical bar with pool tables and such, catering to a somewhat upscale crowd of post-collegiate types. Downstairs, amid many colored candles and soft lighting, is the small stage area. You won't see many big names here, but you won't see any kids fresh out of the garage who can barely play their instruments, either. During the week you'll find occasional theme nights, featuring anything from very cheap local rock showcases, to soul and even swing bands.

Waxman Candles

 3044 N. Lincoln Avenue 773-929-3000
Hours: Mon–Wed, 11 A.M.–7 P.M.; Thu, 11 A.M.–8 P.M.;
Fri, 11 A.M.–7 P.M.; Sat, 11 A.M.–6 P.M.; Sun, 12 P.M.–5 P.M.

This shop produces its very own candles. Here you'll find an endless variety of very good quality candles and holders, from your typical columns and votives to layered and even "spiral" candles. An interesting place.

Army & Navy Surplus

 3100 N. Lincoln Avenue 773-348-8930
Hours: Mon–Fri, 8 A.M.–5 P.M.; Sat, 10 A.M.–5 P.M.

 This is a bit of an odd store as you are not allowed to enter very far past the doorway. What you are supposed to do is window shop outside first, where all the merchandise is on display. The owner then goes and fetches whatever it is you wish to see. So don't take it personally if you forget about these instructions and immediately find yourself the center of attention. The merchandise is strictly military surplus, with no hip concessions such as jeans or blouses. The boot collection is the store's best asset.

Wacky Cats

3012 N. Lincoln Avenue 773-929-6701
Hours: Mon–Tue, 12 P.M.–7 P.M.; Wed, 3 P.M.–7 P.M.;
Fri–Sun, 12 P.M.–7 P.M.

This attractive little boutique offers high-quality vintage clothing. For men there are several mint-condition suits and tuxedos, and for the women many dresses and gowns and a good selection of hats. This is the real stuff, mostly from the '50s on down. Prices are a bit high, but they reflect the quality of the merchandise.

Arriba Mexico

3140 N. Lincoln Avenue 773-281-3939
Hours: Open every day, 9 A.M.–6 A.M.

This Mexican taqueria serves up some of the tastiest chorizo burritos in the city, not to mention scads of other dishes. The dining area is large and usually hopping late at night, the jukebox blasting out your favorite Mexican ditties. And some not so Mexican. Early one evening I was dining away, one of the few people present. The jukebox was playing automatically, randomly selecting tunes. Imagine my surprise when a Sisters of Mercy tune came on. You just never know what the hell to expect in this world, do you?

Euro Cafe

3100 N. Ashland Avenue 773-929-8640
Hours: Open every day, 4 P.M.–12 A.M.

I'm afraid I haven't been here since this place changed its name from Little Bucharest to Euro Cafe, but from what I've heard, it still serves up the same hearty Romanian fare. This stuff is quite good, or at least the beef goulash is, which is what I always ordered. Yeah, I know, I should sample other dishes, but how often do I get Romanian food—of course I've got to go with a classic. But I do know, according to my woman, that the duck is also very good. The decor of this place offers just as much a reason to visit as the food. Stepping into the dim interior, with stained glass windows, it's not hard to imagine you might indeed be in some roadside tavern in the Carpathian Mountains, where fear and superstition reign. Or maybe not. As for myself, however, I like to indulge in such whimsy. Hopefully the place still offers its diners a shot of some strong, unidentifiable liquor, which you drink from a long plastic tube, as if siphoning gas. I imagine this custom probably started up during the Soviet era rather than during Vlad the Impaler's time, but it provides an interesting twist to your meal all the same.

Healing Earth Resources

3111 N. Ashland Avenue 773-327-8459
Hours: Mon–Sat, 10 A.M.–9 P.M.; Sun, 11 A.M.–7 P.M.

This attractive, incense-scented shop features a wide variety of merchandise dealing with spirituality and various New Age philosophies. From books, cassettes, and videos to candles, jewelry, crystals, and greeting cards, this place has a little bit of everything—even a limited selection of clothes. Classes and workshops are also held here, and you can even get a massage or a dose of aromatherapy.

Ark Thrift Shop

3345 N. Lincoln Avenue 773-248-1117
Hours: Mon–Thu, 10 A.M.–6 P.M.; Fri, 10 A.M.–5 P.M.
(summer) 10 A.M.–2 P.M. (winter); Sun, 11 A.M.–5 P.M.

Ah, the second mighty Ark Thrift Shop. This one has three floors and is very well organized. Amid the clothing are many serviceable items scorned by the vintage store pickers such as sweatpants and sweatshirts. The furniture selection is first rate, with many reasonably priced pieces. The bargain basement is much more hit or miss. Tons of books, bicycles, mattresses, and even crutches and walkers are there to greet you.

Record Emporium

3346 N. Paulina Street 773-248-1821
Hours: Mon–Sat, 11 A.M.–7 P.M.; Sun, 12 P.M.–6 P.M.

This comfortable, well-worn shop has a large collection of records, from Bobby Sherman to 7 Seconds to Scandal (featuring Patty Smythe, of course). But they're not for the picky. Most of the albums aren't in the best of shape, but are priced accordingly. There are also plenty of new indie rock CDs, as well as a good selection of used books on music—most of them biographies of rock stars. A pleasant place to spend some time browsing.

Tai's Lounge

3611 N. Ashland Avenue 773-348-8923
Hours: Sun–Fri, 7 P.M.–4 A.M.; Sat, 7 P.M.–5 A.M.

One of the more laid-back bars in Lakeview, Tai's attracts a twenty/thirtysomething clientele, but that's about the only generalization you can make about the place. You'll find all sorts mingling here into the wee hours, from yuppies to hippies and everywhere in between. There are plenty of tables, a good jukebox, and lots of different beers to choose from. If you're in the area, this is one of the best 4 A.M. bars you're likely to find.

Diner Grill

1635 W. Irving Park Road 773-248-2030
Hours: Open 24 hours

It doesn't get much more authentic than this. This is an old diner car that has been in the business of egg-and-hash slinging for many a generation. The food is decent and cheap. If you're feeling brave after a night of drinking, order "The Slinger." I've experienced it once, and though it lives in my memory as exceptionally tasty, I've been too afraid to ever try it again. If I can recall correctly, it's one big platter of food consisting of—one on top of the other—two cheeseburger patties, two fried eggs, hash browns, and chili. I think that's it, though there might be a few more ingredients. Whatever the case, don't eat this if you have any romantic plans for the next day.

13

BOYS TOWN

As you can probably guess from its nickname, this neighborhood is Chicago's gay capital. Gay pride flags and rainbow stickers are visible on many businesses and apartment buildings along Halsted and Broadway, and the city even erected "rainbow columns" a few years back to honor the neighborhood. Here you'll find gay bars that range in style from your typical, upscale neighborhood tavern to clubs with rather unsubtle names such as Manhole. Less concentrated than a place like the Castro in San Francisco, Boys Town has more of the flavor of another storied gay community, the Fauborg-Marigny in New Orleans—only here the population is much more yuppie in outlook and profession. Boys Town, along with its cousins in California and Louisiana, is looked upon as a respectable neighborhood, and an expensive one as well.

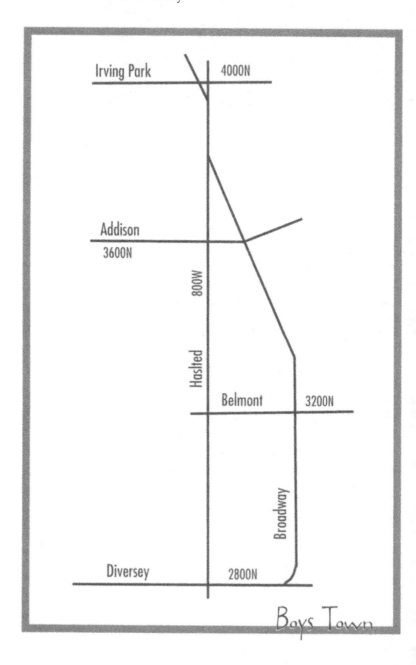

Booklegger's Used Books

2907 N. Broadway Avenue 773-404-8780
Hours: Sun–Thu, 12 P.M.–9 P.M.; Fri–Sat,
12 P.M.–9:30 P.M.

Small but tidy, this place offers a decent, general selection of books as well as CDs and cassettes. The fiction section is their best asset.

Nancy's Original Stuffed Pizza

2930 N. Broadway Avenue 773-883-1977/883-1616
Hours: Sun–Thu, 12 P.M.–12 A.M.; Fri–Sat, 12 P.M.–2 A.M.

This little restaurant whips up one of the best stuffed pizzas in town. This is Chicago-style pizza for real—the slices are so thick and full you won't be able to down more than two pieces at most. In addition to the pizza, they also serve up a variety of sandwiches and pasta dishes—all at reasonable prices.

Discus CD Exchange

2935 N. Broadway Avenue 773-868-0952
Hours: Open every day, 11 A.M.–9 P.M.

This small shop, as the name implies, deals in used CDs. They don't have a huge selection, and the majority of discs are rock, but they do take pains to keep each genre separate and distinct. They also have good deals, such as three CDs for twenty dollars. You can also find a small collection of unremarkable DVD titles.

The Pleasure Chest

XXX *3155 N. Broadway Avenue 773-525-7151*
Hours: Sun–Mon, 12 P.M.–10 P.M.; Tue–Sat, 11 A.M.–12 A.M.

A Chicago institution. This "sex boutique" caters to both gays and heteros with a small assortment of leather accoutrements, porn videos, greeting cards, and various instruments of penetration. Most formidable-looking item: "The Hand"—a life-sized, latex forearm ending in a set of steepled fingers with which you can indulge whatever whim such an item might inspire in you.

Reckless Records

3157 N. Broadway Avenue 773-404-5080
Hours: Mon–Sat, 10 A.M.–10 P.M.; Sun, 10 A.M.–8 P.M.

This store is Reckless' Chicago flagship. Within its spacious interior you'll find an extensive collection of new, used, and rare CDs, vinyl, cassettes, videos, and DVDs as well as fanzines and music mags. In addition they've got T-shirts and a 99¢ CD bargain bin. They also host occasional in-store appearances. Plus, if you're looking to unload any music, this is the place to come. They offer the best prices in town.

Metal Haven

604 W. Belmont Avenue 773-755-9202
Hours: Tue–Thu, 1 P.M.–9 P.M.; Fri–Sat, 12 P.M.–9 P.M.;
Sun, 1 P.M.–6 P.M.

Appropriately named, this is Chicago's premier record shop for metal. Running the gamut in genres, you can find everything here from death metal to plain old hard rock and every shade between, including many genres that I'm not qualified to distinguish between (I used to like some of the better-known "thrash metal" bands, but that's not exactly something that'll endear me to an independent-label metal connoisseur). Both new and used CDs and vinyl can be had here, in addition to T-shirts and magazines. Yes, Metal Haven does indeed have, as they declare, "The most metal at the best price!"

Land of the Lost

614 W. Belmont Avenue 773-529-4966
Hours: Mon–Fri, 12 P.M.–7 P.M.; Sat–Sun, 11 A.M.–7 P.M.

This is a nicely appointed, attractive little shop specializing in vintage clothes, games, and knickknacks. The emphasis is more on kitsch rather than high-fashion, but they do have plenty of serviceable items for the less-flashy dresser. This is in addition to a good selection of albums and old *Playboy* magazines—you may even remember a few centerfolds from your ill-spent youth. Also, the owner's a good guy and the prices are generally cheaper here than in most places in the neighborhood.

Unabridged Books

 3251 N. Broadway Avenue 773-883-9119
Hours: Mon–Fri, 10 A.M.–10 P.M.; Sat–Sun,
10 A.M.–8 P.M.

An attractive, independent store selling new books, Unabridged is one of the few gay-oriented book shops in Chicago. Though they stock plenty of mainstream works and have a nice children's section, their niche is definitely in gay and lesbian writers. They've got quite a large selection.

Borderline Music

 3333 N. Broadway Avenue 773-975-9533
Hours: Mon–Sat, 10 A.M.–8 P.M.; Sun, 11 A.M.–7 P.M.

If you're into club music, this is a good place to come for used CDs. The shop is not geared toward the serious aficionado of dance music, but instead offers a wide variety of artists who have had plenty of play in the clubs over the years. From house and techno to new wave and pop, most of their selection is very radio friendly. One big plus is the large collection of CD singles they offer. Yes, I admit to having fond memories of a couple of Dead or Alive tunes from the '80s ("You spin me right round baby right round . . .") but I certainly wouldn't want to suffer through an entire album. You feel the same way about other bands, I know, so those singles can really come in handy.

Selected Works Bookstore

3510 N. Broadway Avenue 773-975-0002
Hours: Open every day, 12 P.M.–9 P.M.

This cluttered, disheveled basement shop features plenty of nooks and crannies to get lost in as you thumb through the books. The history section is the strongest, though they do have a decent amount of quality fiction. Just make sure you don't accidentally step on the store cat.

Beatnix

3400 N. Halsted Street 773-281-6933
Hours: Mon–Thu, 11 A.M.–10 P.M.; Fri–Sat, 11 A.M.–12 A.M.; Sun, 11 A.M.–9 P.M.

This bright and airy used clothing shop carries plenty of tank-tops, shorts, jeans, and assorted shirts for both men and women, as well as a good collection of black biker leathers. Wigs are also available, only these colorful specimens are not exactly the kind your balding great aunt would wear. In the cluttered basement you'll find more jeans and shirts, but the quality takes a big drop.

99th Floor

3406 N. Halsted Street 773-348-7781
Hours: Mon, 3 P.M.–9 P.M.; Wed–Fri, 3 P.M.–9 P.M.; Sat–Sun, 12 P.M.–10 P.M.

Every gloomy young goth's dream—a boutique just for them! 99th Floor features Chicago's best selection of fashionable goth wear for both men and women. Their boot selection is quite impressive as well. In my younger days (yes, this place has been around forever) I forked over a decent amount of cash here.

Evil Clown Compact Disc

3418 N. Halsted Street 773-472-4761
Hours: Mon–Fri, 12 P.M.–10 P.M.; Sat, 11 A.M.–9 P.M.;
Sun, 12 P.M.–7 P.M.

As the name implies, you won't find anything but CDs here. Selling both new and used, they have a small but decent selection. Rock is the specialty, but they do have a good amount of dance and industrial. And, oddly enough, one of the most thorough collections of Uncle Tupelo I've ever seen, God bless 'em.

Chicago Diner

3411 N. Halsted Street 773-935-6696
Hours: Mon–Thu, 11 A.M.–10 P.M.; Fri, 11 A.M.–11 P.M.;
Sat, 10 A.M.–11 P.M.; Sun, 10 A.M.–10 P.M.

This small, attractive restaurant features Chicago's most-extensive all-vegetarian menu. From simple grain burgers to veggie chili, pasta dishes, and rice-and-bean skillets, there's plenty to choose from—as well as a choice between soy or dairy products. A good beer selection is also available. In the spring and summer a very cozy patio is opened. Though as you certainly know by now I'm not a vegetarian, this food is tasty enough to make you forget meat—at least for a little while. Though it can get a bit expensive, lunching here on a summer afternoon on the patio is a very civilized way to spend an hour or two.

Batteries Not Included

3420 N. Halsted Street 773-935-9900
Hours: Sun–Thu, 11 A.M.–12 A.M.; Fri, 11 A.M.–1 A.M.;
Sat, 10 A.M.–2 A.M.

This little store is one of a handful of Halsted Street sex shops, though this is much more properly a novelty shop. The majority of stock is comprised of nutty little risqué gift items. They do, however, have a small selection of the classics: vibrators, dildos, and oils. They also advertise that 50 percent of their profits go to charity.

Gaymart

3457 N. Halsted Street 773-929-4272
Hours: Mon–Sat, 11 A.M.–7 P.M.; Sun, 11 A.M.–6 P.M.

This small, nook-filled variety store is a lot of fun. It's jam-packed with everything from *Star Wars* memorabilia to rainbow-colored candles, clocks, T-shirts, keychains, and stationery; you can lose quite a bit of time browsing. They also sell the rather expensive but intriguing Billy and Carlos dolls. These are roughly the size of the old Hasbro G.I. Joe dolls and are action figures of the gay kind. Not only could Billy and Carlos serve as a fine companion for G.I. Joe, but—judging by their build—they could out-wrestle him in seconds flat. And Billy and Carlos are, of course, anatomically correct. No pimpled nub in the nether regions for these gentlemen.

Leathersport

XXX
3505 N. Halsted Street 773-868-0914
Hours: Mon–Thu, 11 A.M.–12 A.M.; Fri–Sun, 11 A.M.–1 A.M.

Billing itself as a place for "big bad boys . . . and girls," Leathersport is the sort of porn shop that makes a straight man slightly hesitant to enter. However, the shop is actually quite low-key and browser-friendly. It's the place to go for the practicing S&M aficionado. Alongside mostly gay porn videos and the usual assortment of vibrators and strap-ons, you'll find plenty of leather S&M apparel as well as plenty of strapping and binding devices for whatever manner of immobilization you desire.

Cupid's Treasure

XXX
3519 N. Halsted Street 773-348-3884
Hours: Sun–Thu, 11 A.M.–12 A.M.; Fri–Sat, 11 A.M.–1 A.M.

This "love boutique" is the sort of high-class porn shop that gives porn shops a good name. It's the sort of place you don't feel the least bit guilty entering. Plenty of attractive couples—both hetero and gay—shop here, browsing amid the wide variety of videos, toys, and implements available. Videos are conveniently subdivided into appropriate gay/hetero/S&M/fetish categories, and there are plenty of novelty gift items available.

Flashy Trash

3524 N. Halsted Street 773-327-6900
Hours: Mon–Fri, 12 P.M.–8 P.M.; Sat, 11 A.M.–8 P.M.;
Sun, 12 P.M.–6 P.M.

This three-room boutique carries new and used women's clothing and accessories. Though the name of the place might lead one to think they carry plenty of polyester sun dresses and such, don't be fooled. The stock, for the most part, is very fashionable, high-quality stuff: hipster tracksuits, T-shirts, shorts, sweaters, and clubwear. In back they carry a good selection of vintage dresses that actually are vintage. Prices are steep, but as mentioned, this isn't cheap, hand-me-down stuff.

Brown Elephant Resale Shop

3651 N. Halsted Street 773-549-5943
Hours: Open every day, 11 A.M.–6 P.M.

This huge Brown Elephant, inhabiting what was once a garage, prominently displays pride flags throughout its interior. And let me tell you—the gay community runs the best Brown Elephant in the city. Vintage-shop-quality stuff for resale shop prices can be found among the lengthy aisles here, from sweatshirts and jeans to footwear and furnishings. The albums are all priced cheaply and are even alphabetized, along with the CDs and films. As for the books, the set-up rivals some bookstores I've seen.

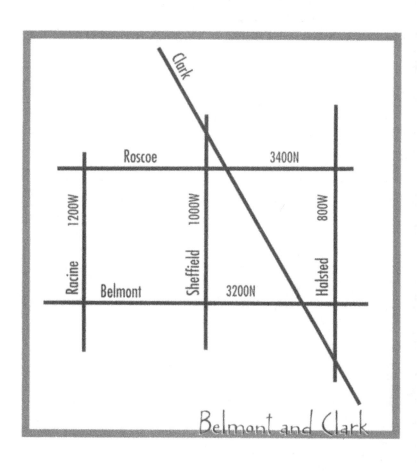

Belmont and Clark

14

BELMONT AND CLARK

Before Chicago's Swedish community thoroughly established themselves in Andersonville around the turn of the century, a number of Swedish families settled in the Belmont/Clark area. Here they could converse in their native tongue and find out about lodging and jobs. Though a hundred years have gone by, the Belmont/Clark area still acts as a magnet, only now it draws teenage suburban hipsters. Back when I was a tender youth of seventeen—and, admittedly, something of a suburban hipster—this was the happening place to be. You would drive straight into the neighborhood from your outlying suburban burg of origin, find a place to park, and then engage in some serious hanging out—or, as the authorities called it, loitering. The legendary juice bar that was the beacon about which we radiated—Club Medusa—is long gone now, but the number of hipster shops catering to the disaffected youth of today has shot through the roof. Indeed, this is the premier "alternative" shopping district in the city. And yes, it is somewhat comforting to see mohawk-sporting youngsters and skinheads still fashionably begging change outside the "Punkin' Donuts" just as they did in my youth.

Of course they are joined now by hordes of scrawny teenagers in clothes many times too big for them or decked-out like funky little goateed versions of Greg Brady, but, over-all, nothing has changed. If anything, the area is more popular than ever.

Sole Junkies

 3176 N. Clark Street 773-529-1944/348-8935
Hours: Mon–Fri, 11 A.M.–8 P.M.; Sun, 12 P.M.–6 P.M.

If you're looking for unique, brand-new hipster footwear—and are willing to fork out a good amount of cash—this is the place to go. Here you'll find a wide selection of clunky-heeled boots and shoes and various hep, brand-name sneakers.

Disc Revival

 3182 N. Clark Street 773-404-4955
Hours: Mon–Sat, 10 A.M.–10 P.M.; Sun, 12 P.M.–7 P.M.

This small used music shop offers a passable selection of music. CDs are not kept rigorously alphabetized; any band starting with the letter *L* is simply lumped into that category in no particular order. This can be a bit annoying if you know what you're looking for, but if you're simply browsing, you end up considering quite a bit of music you otherwise might have ignored. A big plus is the fact that CDs are always $7.99 or less. In addition to the tunes they also sell a smattering of DVDs and video games.

Pink Frog

 3201 N. Clark Street 773-525-2680
Hours: Mon–Sat, 11 A.M.–7:30 P.M.; Sun, 1 P.M.–6 P.M.

This girly shop deals in new clothing and footwear. Much of it is quite hip and could come in handy for clubbing and such, but they do have more mundane offerings for the corporate environment as well. The prices aren't bad either—not as high as you might expect.

Mama Desta's Red Sea Ethiopian Restaurant

3216 N. Clark Street 773-935-7561
Hours: Mon, 4 P.M.–10:30 P.M.; Tue–Thu, 3 P.M.–10:30 P.M.;
Fri–Sun, 11:30 A.M.–11:30 P.M.

As the name tells you, this place serves up Ethiopian food, which I'd never had before eating here years back. I must say I was impressed. Mama Desta's gives you heaping portions of either meat or vegetables—or both—at reasonable prices, all of which are served on platters of spongy bread. And yes, they do have African beer—Mamba, the malt liquor of kings!

Hot Threads

3223 N. Clark Street 773-665-9988
Hours: Mon–Sat, 12 P.M.–9 P.M.; Sun, 12 P.M.–6 P.M.

This is a two-level shop selling a wide variety of new women's clothing, footwear, and accessories. They've got quite a selection, from dresses and jeans to bikinis and "costumes," including a particularly compelling Snow White outfit that would have surprised, intrigued, and no doubt confused the Seven Dwarfs. In fact, most of the apparel here tends toward the slinky and provocative, from near fabric-less miniskirt dresses to those hip hugger jeans that display a generous amount of waist cleavage. (Is that phrase in use? If not, it should be—and I'll take the dubious credit for coining it.) Needless to say, this is not exactly the kind of place a mother would take her daughter to shop, but you do see plenty of teenage boys bringing their girlfriends here. Lucky for them, the prices aren't outrageous. Not cheap, certainly, but not outlandish. The lads can still have money left over to buy their sweetheart a smoothie at the Alternative Shopping Complex, and, perhaps, a pair of skull earrings. Ain't young love sweet?

Secrets

3229 N. Clark Street 773-755-0179
Hours: Mon–Thu, 11:30 A.M.–10:30 P.M.; Fri, 11:30 A.M.–
12 A.M.; Sat, 11:30 A.M.–11:30 P.M.; Sun, 12 P.M.–10 P.M.

This is primarily a head shop, selling a large variety of, ahem, cigarette "holders" and "coolers." In addition, they also sell lingerie and a few (let's stick with the euphemisms) "marital aids."

Two Doors South

3230 N. Clark Street 773-404-7072
Hours: Mon–Thu, 11 A.M.–9 P.M.; Fri–Sat, 11 A.M.–11 P.M.;
Sun, 12 P.M.–8 P.M.

Ah, a place for the inner hippie in all of us. In this tiny shop you'll find plenty of trippy-dippy jewelry, incense, and candles.

The Doc Store

3240 N. Clark Street 773-244-0099
Hours: Mon–Sat, 12 P.M.–8 P.M.; Sun, 12 P.M.–6 P.M.

A Dr. Martin aficionado's dream. This small shop offers a wide selection of the Doctor's finest footwear, not to mention an extensive collection of patches and stickers. Sunglasses, T-shirts, and jewelry are also available.

Shiroi Hana Restaurant

3242 N. Clark Street 773-477-1652
Hours: Mon–Thu, 12 P.M.–2:25 P.M. and 5 P.M.–9:55 P.M.;
Fri–Sat, 5 P.M.–10:25 P.M.; Sun, 4:30 P.M.–9:25 P.M.

This bustling little Japanese restaurant serves up a fine selection of fare, from sushi and your basic teriyaki and tempura dishes to a wide variety of seafood. Prices aren't cheap but they are reasonable and the food is worth it. Another plus is the variety of Japanese beers available. Of course in my limited experience I've found that all Japanese beer tastes the same, but still, in my view, the more beer selections available, the better the restaurant.

Chicago Comics

3244 N. Clark Street 773-528-1983
Hours: Mon–Thu, 12 P.M.–8 P.M.; Fri, 12 P.M.–10 P.M.;
Sat, 11 A.M.–10 P.M.; Sun, 12 P.M.–6 P.M.

Here in this spacious shop you'll find a good collection of small press, import, and adult comics as well as a small bin of back issues—mostly of the superhero ilk. But I have to ask, who buys adult comics? I mean it seems like some of them might be interesting—not to mention "titillating," but would you be more embarrassed to buy an X-rated comic or *Hustler*? Is buying the comic a cop-out or a sign of intellectualism? Hmm . . . anyway, they also carry a number of model kits as well as several offbeat non-fiction books.

Harlequin Treats

3248 N. Clark Street 773-477-7710
Hours: Open every day from 11:30 A.M.–7 P.M., though
opening and closing times sometimes vary by about a
half hour

Consider Harlequin Treats your one-stop shopping destination for collectibles and barbecue sauce. Yes, along with scads of collectibles—everything from stamps and coins to CDs and decorative plates—they carry a wide array of barbecue sauces, marinades, and hot sauces. Interesting, to say the least.

Chicago Music Exchange

3270 N. Clark Street 773-477-0830
Hours: Mon–Fri, 11 A.M.–7 P.M.; Sat, 11 A.M.–6 P.M.

Within the small confines of this place you'll find a great selection of used and vintage guitars and amps. They also do repair work, and are quite nice about it. A friend of mine once brought a guitar in for some work, went out of town, and completely forgot about it. When he returned two months later had they sold it? No. Had they smashed it to bits? No. Did they even charge him a storage fee? No. Noble folks, I tell ya.

Medusa's Circle

 3268 N. Clark Street 773-935-5950
Hours: Mon–Sat, 12 P.M.–8 P.M.; Sun, 1 P.M.–6 P.M.

The place to go for the young femme-fatale goth. This boutique features new, used, and vintage clothing for the doom–and-gloom set. Plenty of black—both in clothes and makeup—to choose from, though they also have many more colorful items, including brand-new "Kangaroo" sneakers—shoes you probably haven't seen since elementary school.

The Honeysuckle Shop

XXX *3326 N. Clark Street 773-529-9700*
Hours: Tue–Sat, 1 P.M.–9 P.M.; Sun, 1 P.M.–6 P.M.

This "sex boutique" is so tastefully done that I could probably bring my mother in here—chances are she wouldn't even realize she was in a sex shop. Selling distinctly "non-seedy" merchandise, this shop is geared toward your average woman, specializing in cleverly disguised vibrators and non-explicit "how-to" manuals and videos, along with oils and lingerie. They even sponsor a weekly "Girls Night Out" in addition to donating some of their proceeds to various women's causes.

Disgraceland

3338 N. Clark Street 773-281-5875
Hours: Mon–Sat, 11 A.M.–7 P.M.; Sun, 12 P.M.–5 P.M.

This new-and-used women's clothing shop doesn't specialize in vintage so much as just plain old modern hipster wear. They carry a decent selection of stuff, including a few men's T-shirts and jeans. They also pay cash for used clothes, so if you're looking to part with any threads, give them a visit.

Hubba-Hubba

3309 N. Clark Street 773-477-1414
Hours: Mon–Sat, 11 A.M.–7 P.M.; Sun, 12 P.M.–5 P.M.

This is a vintage store that lives up to its name. You'll find many items from the '30s and '40s here, most of it for women and most of it expensive. The stock is very elegant and high quality, so paying high prices for this merchandise is not like spending a ridiculous amount of money on an Adidas sweatshirt from the '70. In fact, back one Christmas in the days when I was just out of college and poor(er), I bought my girlfriend an expensive, full-length skirt from here. It was from the '30s and quite elegant. Of course we broke up only a couple of weeks later so I never got to see her wear it, but that's beside the point. Do I regret having tossed all that money Hubba-Hubba's way? Of course not. Did I ever weep over how many cases of Black Label I could have bought with that money? Of course not. Never. Not once. . . .

Hollywood Mirror

812 W. Belmont Avenue 773-404-4510
Hours: Mon–Thu, 11 A.M.–8 P.M.; Fri–Sat, 11 A.M.–9 P.M.;
Sun, 11 A.M.–7 P.M.

Walking into this large, colorful, sunny retro shop kind of makes you feel like you're entering a kaleidoscope. Or at least it made me feel that way once. Of course that could have been due to the contrast between the heat outside and the air-conditioning inside and the resulting head rush I experienced, but whatever the case, you'll find this quite an attractive store. They carry a large selection of jeans, shirts, toys, and lava lamps along with dresses and footwear. In the basement you'll find more clothes as well as vintage kitchen tables straight from the '50s and '60s. Unfortunately, prices are a bit steep, but the merchandise is of good quality. Don't tell them I said so, but even if you don't want to drop any dough, this place is still worth visiting for the ambience alone.

Ragstock

812 W. Belmont Avenue, 2nd floor 773-868-9263
Hours: Mon–Thu, 10 A.M.–9 P.M.; Fri–Sat, 10 A.M.–10 P.M.;
Sun, 12 P.M.–8 P.M.

This is the first store Ragstock opened in Chicago. Located above Hollywood Mirror, this large, spacious shop is a favorite with the kids, both male and female. Amid the racks are many new and used dresses, tank tops, jeans, T-shirts, and footwear—along with an extensive selection of camouflage pants. Most of the stock is fairly expensive, yet here and there are many good deals—such as new T-shirts for only $3.50. They might not survive more than two washes, but hey, what do you expect at that price?

The Alley a.k.a The Alternative Shopping Complex

858 W. Belmont Avenue 773-883-1800
Hours: Mon–Thu, 11 A.M.–10 P.M.; Fri–Sat, 11 A.M.–12 A.M.;
Sun 12 P.M.–9 P.M.

Historians like to compare the modern shopping mall to Medieval cathedrals in terms of the social impact they have on the surrounding community. Much like the dirt-floored shack of a church that eventually metamorphosed into a spectacular cathedral, so too has The Alley grown from its humble origins as a small, cluttered head shop on Broadway. It is now a mini-mall of its own, and like the cathedrals of old, it weekly draws hundreds of dedicated, youthful pilgrims from the city and suburbs who quiver in fits of materialistic ecstasy once they enter. The complex is located in the big building that looms behind the Dunkin Donuts on the northwestern corner of Clark and Belmont, though some of the affiliated shops have left the nest and spread to adjacent storefronts on both of those streets. Here amid these various shops you'll find everything from gothic clubwear to T-shirts, jewelry, footwear, leather jackets, plaster columns and gargoyles, music and films, cigars and humidors, lingerie, condoms, vibrators, and even whips and swords (yes, whips and swords). None of it is particularly cheap, but even if you're not looking to buy anything, The Alley "empire" is definitely worth a visit.

Egor's Dungeon

900 W. Belmont Avenue 773-525-7131
Hours: Mon–Thu, 11:30 A.M.–10:30 P.M.;
Fri–Sat, 11:30 A.M.–12 A.M.; Sun, 11:30 A.M.–10 P.M.

This small shop is a combination head shop/porn shop. The selection is fairly limited, but they do have a nice collection of bowls. A few whips, some items of lingerie, and a smattering of porno videos and vibrators flesh things out, so to speak.

Philly's Best

907 W. Belmont Avenue 773-525-7900
Hours: Mon–Thu, 11 A.M.–12 A.M.; Fri–Sat, 11 A.M.–2 A.M.;
Sun, 12 P.M.–9 P.M.

This fast-food joint bills itself as the best place outside Philadelphia to get cheese steak sandwiches. Well, having been to Philly a number of times in the past few years—where, of course, I've dutifully gobbled down plenty of cheesesteaks—I find little to quibble about in such a claim. Their other sandwiches—which are baked and called "oven grinders"—are huge and tasty as well. They also serve pizza and salads. Not exactly cheap, but you definitely get more than your money's worth.

The Chicago Tattooing & Piercing Company

922 W. Belmont Avenue 773-528-6969
Hours: Open every day, 12 P.M.–12 A.M.

In business since the mid-'60s, this is Chicago's oldest tattoo parlor—and, as they claim, the best. Not having any tattoos myself, I can't vouch for the place personally, but a friend of mine got a tattoo here and was quite pleased with the craftsmanship and procedure, which jibes with the good word-of-mouth reputation this place has always enjoyed "on the street," if I may be so bold as to use such a phrase. Keep in mind, however, that they don't even want to see you walking through the door unless you're over eighteen.

The Gallery Bookstore

923 W. Belmont Avenue 773-975-8200
Hours: Mon–Fri, 1 P.M.–8 P.M.; Sat, 12 P.M.–8 P.M.;
Sun, 12 P.M.–7 P.M.

This was once a cramped little warren on Broadway. Now it's a cramped little warren on Belmont, albeit a less confusing one. You can't get lost in this one. What you'll find is a well-organized, general selection of fiction and nonfiction intermingled with many well-kept rarities. I just hope you're not claustrophobic.

Record Exchange

925 W. Belmont Avenue 773-975-9285
Hours: Mon–Sat, 11 A.M.–10 P.M.; Sun, 11 A.M.–7 P.M.

In this comfortable, laid-back shop you'll find a decent selection of both new and used CDs as well as an extensive collection of cassettes and vinyl. As for the vinyl, we're not just talking about seventies rock. They carry a prodigious amount of jazz, blues, country, and even classical.

Tragically Hip

931 W. Belmont Avenue 773-549-1500
Hours: Mon–Sat, 11 A.M.–7 P.M.; Sun, 11 A.M.–6 P.M.

Yep, the name says it all. This is, indeed, a retro clothing store. Bet you couldn't have guessed. Catering mostly to women, this place stocks more conventional, expensive stuff. The place to go if you want stylish, hip clothing that can be worn at the office.

Belmont Army Surplus

945 W. Belmont Avenue 773-549-1038
Hours: Mon–Sat, 11 A.M.–8 P.M.; Sun, 1 P.M.–6 P.M.

This place has come a long way from the days when
the clerks used to reprimand you for poking through a
stack of jeans. In fact, upon entering you'll think the
sign out front misleading. The first floor is given over
entirely to pricey, brand-new hipster wear—both
clothing and footwear. Upstairs, however, you'll find a
wide variety of army surplus gear as well as an extensive collection of leather jackets. And the clerks, I
might add, are now friendly.

Never Mind

953 W. Belmont Avenue 773-472-4922
Hours: Mon–Sat, 11 A.M.–8 P.M.; Sun, 11:30 A.M.–5:30 P.M.

Kind of an odd name for a women's clothing store,
don't you think? Anyway, within its confines you'll find
a wide variety of affordable dresses, blouses, and
shirts, and footwear. These range in style from the
near-conservative to hoity-toity club wear. Strangely
enough, I've even found a couple of dirt-cheap, brand-
new pairs of men's long underwear pants here. Happy
hunting.

Berlin

954 W. Belmont Avenue 773-348-4975
Hours: Mon, 8 P.M.–4 A.M.; Tue–Fri, 5 P.M.–4 A.M.;
Sat, 5 P.M.–5 A.M.; Sun, 6 P.M.–4 A.M.

This nightclub has been a Chicago institution for
many a long year and is one of the city's best known
lesbian bars—though, of course, they advertise that
they cater to "every sexuality." And indeed, they even
have a "Boys' Night." Dark and smoky inside, Berlin is
the place to go if you're looking to wiggle about on a
dance floor.

Muskie's

 963 W. Belmont Avenue 773-477-1880
Hours: Mon–Thu, 11 A.M.–2 A.M.; Fri–Sat, 11 A.M.–4 A.M.;
Sun, 11 A.M.–12 A.M.

Muskie's is one of the better traditional fast-food joints in town, with a wide range of items to pick from including burgers, gyros, and hot wings. What really sets it apart, though, are the number of vegetarian entrées on the menu. The fries are damn good too. They're of the skinny variety, the kind of critters you can pop into your mouth ten at a time.

Leona's Restaurant

3215 N. Sheffield Avenue 773-327-8861
Hours: Sun–Thu, 11 A.M.–12 A.M.; Fri–Sat, 11 A.M.–1 A.M.

This is the restaurant that started it all. From here the Leona's empire was able to expand throughout the city. As I've mentioned before and as you'll no doubt read again in upcoming pages, for my money Leona's makes the best thin-crust pizza in Chicago. The rest of the menu is no slouch either, from huge specialty sandwiches to pasta and seafood dishes. As for the restaurant itself, your dining experience will be casual, fun, and—considering this is one of their busier locations—loud and somewhat crowded as well. All the same, I'm sure you'll find the food very much worth it.

Sheffield's Wine and Beer Garden

3258 N. Sheffield Avenue 773-281-4989
Hours: Mon–Fri, 2 P.M.–2 A.M.; Sat, 12 P.M.–3 A.M.;
Sun, 12 P.M.–2 A.M.

A place like Sheffield's is very hard to find in this neighborhood. Though it regularly gets quite crowded and loud, the bar always retains a low-key, relaxed atmosphere. The patrons tend to be a bit more "artsy" than the crowds you'll find at most area bars, and the place even sports a back room where small drama productions are occasionally staged. More pluses: dozens of beers, paintings by local artists, and one of the most attractive beer gardens in town—they even have a pool table set up in it. The most unusual attraction here, however, is the enormously fat cat that roams the top of the bar at will, casually winding his way amid the glasses and bottles to his water bowl at the far end—a gigantic martini glass. Then again, considering how fat he is and how often you'll find him lapping away, that glass just might not be filled with water.

Saturday Audio Exchange

1021 W. Belmont Avenue 773-935-4434
Hours: Thu, 5:30 P.M.–9 P.M.; Sat, 10:30 A.M.–5:30 P.M.;
Sun, 12 P.M.–4 P.M.

This is a great place to go if you're looking for used audio equipment. Though they do carry some new gear, you'll find the used stuff is of very high quality, selling at excellent prices. From turntables to home theater systems, they've got it all. Considering the select hours of operation, the place is usually packed, but the staff is consistently helpful and knowledgeable.

Moti Mahal Indian Restaurant

1031 W. Belmont Avenue 773-348-4392
Hours: Sun–Thu, 12 P.M.–9:30 P.M.;
Fri–Sat, 12 P.M.–10:30 P.M.

This small, casual restaurant (don't let the linen on the tables fool you), serves up a large variety of curries and other Indian dishes. The food won't make you swoon with ecstasy, but it is good, appetizing fare. Here you can also purchase jewelry and undiluted patchouli oil along with Indian videos and DVDs.

Something Old Something New

1056 W. Belmont Avenue 773-271-1300
Hours: Mon–Fri, 9 A.M.–9 P.M.; Sat–Sun, 9 A.M.–8 P.M.

This huge shop carries both used and new clothing at very reasonable prices. They have plenty of jeans, shirts, dresses—you name it. You probably won't find any big-name brands or exceedingly funky apparel, but for average, no-nonsense clothing, this place is perfect.

15

WRIGLEYVILLE

Still a somewhat sketchy neighborhood only twenty years ago, Wrigleyville is now one of the more popular neighborhoods in the city, the blue-collar whites who once owned homes in the area having been replaced by white professionals and their large dogs. The home of the Chicago Cubs—Wrigley Field—is the main draw, of course, but there are plenty of bars, clubs, restaurants, and shops dotting the area to keep people busy in the off-season, including quite a few Japanese eateries. For most city-dwellers, Wrigleyville long ago replaced Rush and Division as the city's premier party destination, and on nights after Cubs games, an almost Bourbon Street/*Animal House* atmosphere pervades the neighborhood.

Pick Me Up Cafe

3408 N. Clark Street 773-248-6613
Hours: Mon–Thu, 5 P.M.–3 A.M.; Opens Fri,
5 P.M. and closes Sun, 3 A.M.

A great place for those who like to brace themselves late at night with some coffee, this colorful, comfortable cafe serves up food and joe throughout the wee hours. A good place to stop on the way home after

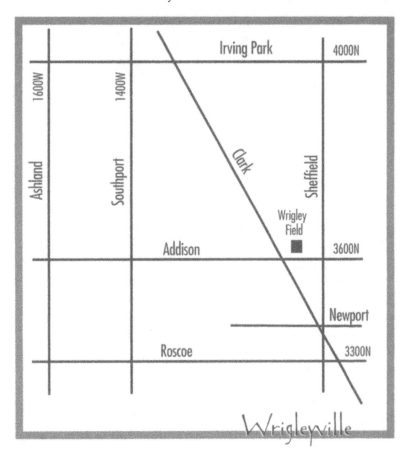

drinking if you can feel a hangover looming in your immediate future.

The Bookworks

3444 N. Clark Street 773-871-5318
Hours: Mon–Thu, 12 P.M.–10 P.M.; Fri-Sat, 12 P.M.–11 P.M.;
Sun, 12 P.M.–6 P.M.

This is one of my favorite used bookstores, but then I'm a bit partial to this joint since I used to work here years ago. The owners, Bob and Ronda, are good people and the overall selection is great—especially the fiction and art sections. They also have plenty of albums, CDs, and some cassettes. In addition to all the used stuff, you'll also find an extensive collection of new books by Kerouac, Bukowski, and Burroughs.

Strange Cargo

3448 N. Clark Street 773-327-8090
Hours: Mon–Sat, 11:30 A.M.–6:45 P.M.;
Sun, 12 P.M.–5:30 P.M.

This sunny, good-sized shop has a decent stock of typical vintage-shop clothes for men and women as well as an extensive selection of leathers, shoes, and jeans. And plenty of fedoras—the perfect accessory for any well-dressed man or woman.

Underground Lounge

952 W. Newport Avenue 773-327-2739
Hours: Sun–Fri, 8 P.M.–2 A.M.; Sat, 8 P.M.–3 A.M.

This intimate basement location has played host to a number of fine clubs over the years, and Underground Lounge continues that tradition. Here you'll find good drink specials throughout the week, with DJs spinning Thursdays and Fridays. Live bands play on Saturdays, ranging in style from rock to jazz and everything in between.

Wrigley Field

1060 W. Addison Street 773-404-2827
Hours: Varies depending on game time; check paper or call.

Need I even mention that this place is a Chicago institution? One of the better-known historical ballparks in the country, Wrigley Field is a pleasant place to pass an afternoon or evening. The bleachers are still pretty cheap, while the entertainment value of the various "bleacher bums" in the stands is priceless. Since Sammy Sosa's monster home-run stretch in '98, attendance has generally been up, therefore don't expect the solitude most hardcore Cub fans have traditionally enjoyed during weekday afternoons. This is especially true in the wake of the Cubs' 2003 playoff run and should continue for some time no matter how badly the team manages to screw things up in the future. Regardless of the team's fortunes, Wrigley Field is full of personality and amusing fans, unlike the horrific, mall-like travesty that is the new Comiskey Park (oh, sorry, U.S. Cellular Field) in Bridgeport where the Sox play. If you're in town in spring or summer, taking in a game at Wrigley is well worth it.

Yesterday

1143 W. Addison Street 773-248-8087
Hours: Mon–Sat, 1 P.M.–7 P.M.; Sun, 2 P.M.–6 P.M.

This weathered, tattered place carries just the sort of merchandise you'd expect from its façade. Inside you'll find plenty of old, dog-eared *Life* magazines, posters, paperbacks, comics, and an extensive collection of sports cards. They even have an O. J. Simpson card. Ah, O. J. Simpson. As a kid, he was the guy I most wanted to emulate. Of course, being white and losing whatever speed I had by the age of twelve made this hopeless. Still though, that's kind of the story of my life: my boyhood hero turned out to be a double-murdering creep.

The Wild Hare & Singing Armadillo Frog Sanctuary

3530 N. Clark Street 773-327-4273
Hours: Sun–Fri, 8 P.M.–2 A.M.; Sat, 8 P.M.–3 A.M.

A Chicago institution, the Wild Hare is Chicago's premier, long-enduring reggae club. DJs and bands are featured throughout the week. In the summer this place gets crowded and hot—not to mention smoky. They also feature occasional Cubs game-day parties with no cover charge. A great, convivial place.

Hi-Fi Records

3728 N. Clark Street 773-388-3838
Hours: Open seven days a week, 12 P.M.–8 P.M. on days
when there are no Metro shows; 12 P.M.–10:30 P.M. on
days when there are shows.

Though the name and management changes, this spot
has always functioned as some sort of hipster record
or book store. A branch of the Hi-Fi Records store in
Lincoln Park now calls this space home. Like the
Lincoln Park store, this incarnation sports plenty of
new, used, and rare vinyl, as well CDs and videos. You
can also buy tickets to shows at Metro next door—free
of service charges.

Metro

3730 N. Clark Street 773-549-0203
Hours: varies depending on show—rarely open before
6 P.M. and never open past 2 A.M.

A Chicago institution (yes, there are many of them in
Wrigleyville), the Metro has been the city's premier
music venue for years. Big enough to host major
national and international acts, the space is also intimate enough that no such thing as a bad seat exists.
Acts as varied as Smashing Pumpkins, The Orb, and
David Lee Roth have graced its stage, but for the most
part the booking pendulum swings solidly to the side
of Smashing Pumpkins and their ilk (on a much
smaller scale of course—the Pumpkins can only play
special shows here these days). This is in addition to
plenty of local bands. Beer prices are ridiculous, so
you should fill up at the Gingerman Tavern before-
hand.

Smart Bar

3730 N. Clark Street, lower level 773-549-0203
Hours: Tue–Fri, 10 P.M.–4 A.M.; Sat, 10 P.M.–5 A.M.;
Sun, 10 P.M.–4 A.M.

Smart Bar is located below Metro, and although
Metro's bouncers herd you here after their perfor-

mances end, Smart Bar is definitely a "progressive" club in its own right. It is, you might say—though I'm sure you're getting sick of hearing this by now—a Chicago institution. The interior has gotten itself a bit of a glossy makeover, but this is still a worthwhile place to wander down into for both dancing and people-watching. I'd advise you to lay off the mind-enhancing drugs for your visit, however. Smart Bar can be a bit of a meat market, and in bouts of heightened consciousness the desperate courting rituals taking place all around you are only apt to fill you with sorrow and pity for the damnable human race. Stick to the alcohol—that way you don't have to feel any shame until morning over your own pathetic attempts to get laid.

Wrigleyville Dogs

3737 N. Clark Street 773-296-1500
Hours: Open every day, 8 A.M.–4 A.M.

What can I say? This typical hot dog and burger joint is directly across the street from Metro, and therefore can come in handy before, during, or after shows.

The Gingerman Tavern

3740 N. Clark Street 773-549-2050
Hours: Mon–Fri, 3 P.M.–2 A.M.; Sat, 12 P.M.–3 A.M.;
Sun, 12 P.M.–2 A.M.

The Gingerman is one of those bars that features an entirely eclectic crowd. From yuppies to rockers, Cub fans to artists, you'll find any and all sorts here. A loud, friendly place, this is a decent joint in which to down a few or shoot some pool.

Nuts on Clark

3830 N. Clark Street 773-549-6622
Hours: Mon–Sat, 9 A.M.–4 P.M.

You don't see too many stores like this one. It's a virtual nut warehouse—of the edible variety, of course. Here you can buy bags of peanuts, pistachios, walnuts, chocolate-covered peanuts—you name it. They also have plenty of gift items such as candy and peanut baskets and such. A cool place.

Brown Elephant Resale Shop

3939 N. Ashland Avenue 773-244-2930
Hours: Open every day, 11 A.M.–6 P.M.

You know the score by now. The Brown Elephant "franchise" features a good selection of clothing, furniture, housewares, music, film—and more! This store isn't as impressive as their Wicker Park and Boys Town locations, but a visit will prove well worth your while.

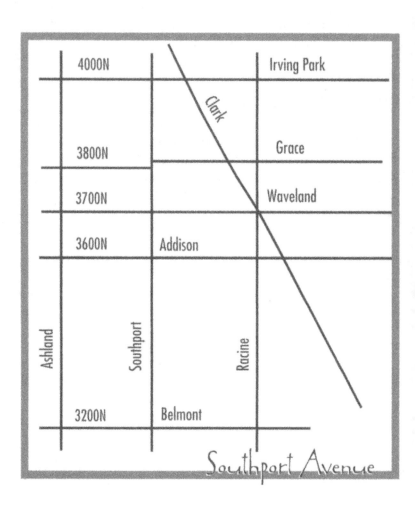

16

SOUTHPORT AVENUE

Though Southport Avenue has become gentrified just like the rest of Lakeview, the speed with which this gentrification took place was astonishing. Back in 1989, I was living on Roscoe just west of Southport. A few blocks west of Clark Street and Wrigley Field, this was a quiet, pleasant, residential neighborhood composed primarily of blue-collar whites along with a small number of Mexican families. Southport Avenue was one of the main commercial strips of the neighborhood, with mom–and-pop department, hardware, and convenience stores running its length; here and there an upscale establishment had popped up, but these were very much in the minority. There was one particular pizza joint near the "L" station that I used to frequent. During the summer months it was very hot and muggy inside—an immense floor fan in the doorway serving as the only air-conditioning. The men in dirty aprons dripping sweat behind the counter were all middle-aged and had the air of taciturn drifters about them. The place was called something like Belli's, and the pizza was bland but edible. It was over the summer when things started changing, with a majority of the old businesses being supplanted by new, yuppified boutiques and cafes. Belli's went out of business with the rest of them. However, a month later it was reopened, still called Belli's. Only now it had been thoroughly remodeled and yuppified. Even so, the same cooks were behind the counter, looking even more dissolute and uncomfortable in their colorful new uniforms. I now became aware of the legend of "Mama Belli." Mama Belli, it turns out, was a much beloved grandmother who had perfected her pizza recipe in the old country using only the finest, freshest ingredients. The Belli family took immense pride in offering her pizza to you, the honored customer, as they had been doing for a number of generations. Or so claimed the slick new take-out menu. Whatever the case, Belli's still turned out the same bland but edible pizza, only now it cost $3 more a pie. My point? Well, I'm not so sure I've actually got one, except to say that Southport Avenue is an extreme case of what can happen to a neighborhood in a very short period of time. Once word gets out about that "hot" new area in which to invest, nothing is safe. But that's life and, I suppose, progress. Southport now boasts a variety of trendy eateries, cafes, and boutiques, catering to the white professionals who have replaced the blue-collar families.

Schubas Tavern

3159 N. Southport Avenue 773-525-2508
Hours: Mon–Fri, grill, 11 A.M.–11 P.M., bar, 2 P.M.–2 A.M.;
Sat, grill, 8 A.M.–11 P.M., bar, 11 A.M.–3 A.M.;
Sun, grill, 9 A.M.–11 P.M., bar, 11 A.M.–2 A.M.

Schubas is one of the better spots in the city to see live bands. Years back the acts were predominantly country-tinged, but straight-up rock bands are a major part of the line-up these days. The one common denominator is quality. You're not likely to see too many bad bands play here, whether local or national. Separate from the main bar, the music area is quite intimate, sporting a good-sized stage and an excellent sound system. The Harmony Grill, adjacent to the bar, serves up hearty, "down home" fare. Their breakfast menu on weekends is particularly good.

Uncle Fun

 1338 W. Belmont Avenue 773-477-8223
Hours: Tue–Fri, 12 P.M.–7 P.M.; Sat, 11 A.M.–7 P.M.;
Sun, 11 A.M.–5 P.M.

Located just east of Schubas on Belmont, Uncle Fun has been around for some twenty years now, and is a great place to visit. Here you'll find scads of toys and novelty items, from jack-in-the-boxes to robots and cymbal-crashing monkeys to fart powder and "Millionaires in Space" figurines. All of which, I should add, is very reasonably priced. If you're in the area, you have to check this place out. Scratch that, you have to check this place out even if you're not in the area. You'll have more fun than a barrel of monkeys—and you can even bring a barrel of monkeys home with you too.

Wisteria

 3715 N. Southport Avenue 773-880-5868
Hours: Thu–Fri, 4 P.M.–9 P.M.; Sat, 12 P.M.–9 P.M.;
Sun, 12 P.M.–5 P.M.

Expensive used and vintage women's, men's and even children's clothes and accessories are the name of the game here. The sort of place you can shop for modern, everyday wear as opposed to many such shops where kitsch is the main selling point.

Music Box Theatre

3733 N. Southport Avenue 773-871-6604
Hours: Varies; check paper or call for showtimes.

One of the premier independent cinemas in Chicago, the Music Box features the finest in contemporary independent releases from all over the world. The main theater harks back to the gilded movie palaces of old and is definitely the most attractive theater you're likely to see in this age of the cineplex. The Music Box also offers midnight screenings of various cult films as well as special showings of old classics.

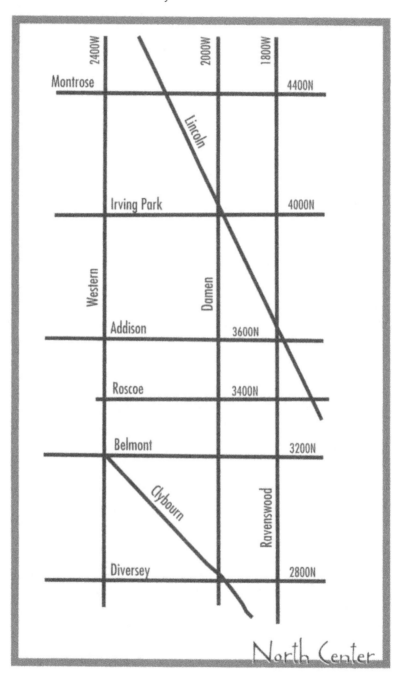

North Center

17

NORTH CENTER

From the early 1900s up to 1968 North Center played host to Riverview, which billed itself as the world's largest amusement park. What will you find in its place now? A strip mall, of course. The amusement park was really the only exciting thing about North Center, which has been primarily residential ever since the first white ethnics began moving out this way in the 1800s. Outside of the commercial strip along Western Avenue, you'll find quiet streets and mixed-income housing. Like the old days, many of the residents are of working-class stock, only now Koreans and Latinos live alongside the whites. There are a few pockets of a more exciting nature in North Center, however. Roscoe Village, St. Ben, and Lincoln Square are three "sub" neighborhoods within the area's boundaries which are described in detail in subsequent chapters. Outside of these particular 'hoods, not a whole lot is going on. Unless, of course, you're into car dealerships and fast-food franchises.

Galaxy Comic Zone

3804 N. Western Avenue 773-267-1043
Hours: Mon–Fri, 12:30 P.M.–7 P.M.; Sat, 11 A.M.–7 P.M.;
Sun, 12:30 P.M.–5:30 P.M.

A nice shop. Here you can get plenty of new comics by the big fellas (Marvel, D.C.) as well as a decent selection of independents. The back issue selection is passable, leaning mainly toward the superheros.

Variety Comics

4602 N. Western Avenue 773-334-2550
Hours: Mon–Sat, 12 P.M.–5 P.M.; Sun, 12 P.M.–4 P.M.

This small basement shop also features the mainstream new titles out there in the comic world, but—unlike many comic shops in the city—they have a great selection of back issues as well. And what I especially like about the place are all the old issues they carry of my youthful favorite—*CONAN!* Oh, the hours I'd spend as a flabby, timid, prepubescent youth wishing that I, too, could be like this steel-thewed barbarian of the north. But let's not resurrect those grim memories.

18

ROSCOE VILLAGE

R oscoe Village, a sub-neighborhood of North Center, perfectly mirrors the changes its neighbor directly to the east, Lakeview, has gone through in population shift. What had once primarily been a neighborhood of blue-collar whites is now filling up with white professionals, though it remains a pleasant, quiet, residential area. You'll find a number of antique stores along Belmont, and on the main strip of Roscoe just west of Damen, a handful of low-key, upscale taverns, cafes, and eateries.

Vintage Deluxe

1846 W. Belmont Avenue 773-529-7008
Hours: Open every day, 11 A.M.–6 P.M.

 This vintage shop is indeed deluxe, as you can get everything here from high-quality furniture and clothing to eyeglasses and footwear. And that's not all. They also carry a great selection of local and national rockabilly bands on CD and vinyl, so not only is this a great place to pick up some high-end old furnishings for the house, but you can keep abreast of what's happening in the rockabilly scene as well. A fine combination indeed.

Roscoe Village

Beat Kitchen

2100 W. Belmont Avenue 773-281-4444
Hours: Sun–Fri, 11:30 A.M.–2 A.M.; Sat, 11:30 A.M.–3 A.M.

This two-story, upscale neighborhood tavern is a pleasant place to down a few micro-brews at the bar or see a local band in the back room. Music is featured nightly, with both local and national acts, though the latter are usually unknown except in indie rock circles. The kitchen churns out high-class bar food, from homemade pizza to burgers and gourmet Italian sausage sandwiches featuring the heftiest shaft of sausage you're ever apt to see on a roll.

Night and Day Vintage

2252 W. Belmont Avenue 773-327-4045
Hours: Wed–Sun, 2 P.M.–7 P.M.

This small vintage shop has a nice collection of dresses and jackets for women and men, along with various

housewares and knicknacks. Some of this stuff goes
back to the '20s and is pretty high-quality stuff.

Hungry Brain

2319 W. Belmont Avenue 773-935-2118
Hours: Tue–Fri, 8 P.M.–2 A.M.; Sat, 8 P.M.–3 A.M.;
Sun, 8 P.M.–2 A.M.

This is a quiet, low-key, neighborhood pub. Here you'll
find a great jukebox, friendly bartenders, and a laid-
back crowd. For you poets out there, they host readings twice a month on the first and third Wednesdays,
with an open mike. This is a great place to sit and converse, for not only can you hear yourself talk, but the
cheap drink prices help fuel the yapping.

Shangrila

1952 W. Roscoe Street 773-348-5090
Hours: Mon–Fri, 12 P.M.–7 P.M.; Sat, 12 P.M.–6 P.M.;
Sun, 12 P.M.–5 P.M.

Small in floor space and selection, Shangrila still manages to boast quite a nice stock. In addition to the
usual vintage dresses, coats, and clothing, you can flip
through mint-condition magazine ads from the '50s
on up. The book section, though relatively small, is
alphabetized and full of cheap, quality literature and
nonfiction—the best of any vintage shop I've seen.

Stern's Books

2004 W. Roscoe Street 773-883-5100
Hours: Tue–Fri, 10 A.M.–6 P.M.; Sat, 10 A.M.–4 P.M.

Though I can't say I would entirely agree with the
proclamation modestly scripted on the storefront that
this is the world's greatest bookstore, I will admit that
Stern's is quite a good one—for psychology. This is
Stern's speciality. The shelves are chock full of books
on psychological theory, teaching methods, and various disorders. There's also quite a bit of child development material, including games and a few toys.

Kitsch'n

2005 W. Roscoe Street 773-248-7372
Hours: Tue–Sat, 9 A.M.–10 P.M.; 9 A.M.–3 P.M.

This retro restaurant is set up just like a prefab suburban '70s kitchen, with plenty of period artifacts (Mr.
Potatohead, lava lamps, etc.) strewn about. The menu
serves up very tasty American classics like chili and
fried chicken. The brunch crowd on weekends is
always heavy, and why not? Where else can you get
green eggs and ham? This joint is particularly nice to
hit in the warmer months, when you can sit out on the
sidewalk or in the beer garden.

Hard Boiled Records and Video

2008 W. Roscoe Street 773-755-2619
Hours: Mon–Sat, 12 P.M.–9 P.M.; Sun, 12 P.M.–6 P.M.

This little shop has a bit of everything. Old and new
comics, offbeat books, videos and DVDs, graphic novels, albums, CDs, and cassettes. The Hong Kong video
section is their specialty, with plenty of fast-paced,
kitschy thrillers in stock for both sale and rental, along
with a number of Korean and Indian titles as well.
Other than the Hong Kong films you won't find a huge
stock of any one particular medium, but there's definitely plenty of quality stuff here.

Village Discount Outlet

2043 W. Roscoe Street
Hours: Mon–Fri, 9 A.M.–9 P.M.; Sat, 9 A.M.–6 P.M.;
Sun, 11 A.M.–5 P.M.

This one is pleasant and actually somewhat sunny
inside, unlike your typical Village Discount. Not to
say you'll find many treasures here, but you know my
policy.

A. J.'s Posters & Prints

2225 W. Roscoe Street 773-388-2276
Hours: Mon–Tue, 10 A.M.–6 P.M.; Thu–Fri, 10 A.M.–6 P.M.;
Sat, 10 A.M.–5 P.M.; Sun, 10 A.M.–3 P.M.

If you're in the market for old concert or movie posters—not to mention art prints—this is your place. The concert posters are the highlight, stretching all the way back to the '60s, in both originals and reprints. The movie prints are heavy on mainstream films, but there are a number of more "out there" selections like *Taste the Blood of Dracula!* For art prints you can choose from a wide variety, from Monet to Warhol. They also do custom framing.

Mojoe's Cafe Lounge

2256 W. Roscoe Street 773-388-1236
Hours: Mon–Fri, 6:30 A.M.–10 P.M.; Sat–Sun,
7:30 A.M.–10 P.M.

This is a cozy little place, set up almost like a "kitchenette" apartment. Here you can get your coffee fix as well as down a smoothie or two. Poetry readings are hosted every now and then, and *Simpsons* viewing parties are a feature on Sundays. They play some great music too.

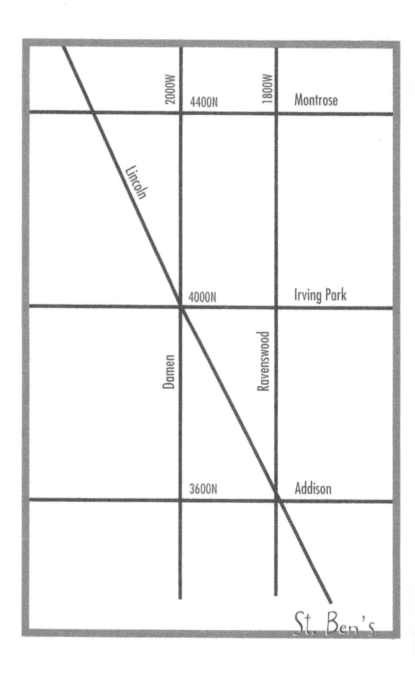

19

ST. BEN'S

Named for St. Benedict's Parish and the church built here in 1904, St. Ben's is a quiet, pleasant North Center neighborhood comprised mostly of white homeowners. Germans were the predominant group here originally, and you'll find a few vestiges of this in a handful of establishments.

Resi's Bierstube

2034 W. Irving Park Road 773-472-1749
Hours: Mon–Fri, 3 P.M.–2 A.M.; Sat,
3 P.M.–3 A.M.; Sun, 3 P.M.–1 A.M.

Whether you're looking to drink or eat—or, preferably, both—Resi's is a great choice. Plenty of German beers are on tap, with dozens more in bottles. The warm-weather months are a particularly a good time to visit, for you can sample several weiss beers while kicking back in the beer garden. For food, you can gulp down hearty brats and knackwurst, as well as wienershnitzel. Even the sauerkraut and German potato salad are excellent. And to top it off, the prices are cheap. *Germany uber alles!*

Deadwax

3819 N. Lincoln Avenue 773-529-1932
Hours: Tue-Fri, 12 P.M.–9 P.M.; Sat, 11 A.M.–9 P.M.;
Sun, 11 A.M.–8 P.M.

This is a quality used record shop. Within this small space is a large collection of vinyl, along with a limited but good selection of CDs. In addition you'll also find videos and DVDs.

Kool Thing

3821 N. Lincoln Avenue 773-327-2738
Hours: Tue–Fri, 1 P.M.–7 P.M.; Sat, 12 P.M.–6 P.M.;
Sun, 12 P.M.–5 P.M.

This attractive little shop features a whole slew of, well, cool things. If you're looking for finely crafted, decorative housewares and jewelry, this is a good place to come. They also have plenty of items etched with the likeness of those cool Mexican skeletons. Okay, I'm showing my cultural ignorance, but you know those Day of the Dead skeletons? That's what I'm talking about. I'm sure there's a folk art term for them that I should use, but I just ain't bright enough to know what it might be.

Grizzly's Lodge

3832 N. Lincoln Avenue 773-281-5112
Hours: Sun–Fri, 11 A.M.–2 A.M.; Sat, 11 A.M.–3 A.M.

Been craving an ostrich burger? How about an elk steak? Well crave no more, friend, you can get all that and more at Grizzly's Lodge. Decked out like a Wisconsin Dells tourist trap, Grizzly's serves up a great selection of traditional bar food along with steaks, ribs, and, of course, wild game. From venison goulash to wild boar chops to buffalo meat loaf, this is the place to chomp down your favorite animal of the forest. They also have a good selection of beers, with nightly specials. If you're looking for something a little different to fill up the innards, this is definitely a fun place to hit.

Martyr's Restaurant & Pub

3855 N. Lincoln Avenue 773-404-9494
Hours: Mon–Fri, 5 P.M.–2 A.M., Sat, 5 P.M.–3 A.M.;
Sun, 10 A.M.–2 A.M.

For the longest time I assumed Martyr's was cursed. Back when I first moved into the city many a long year ago, the building Martyr's occupies was owned by the Moderne Card Co. I telemarketed for this outfit for a few months and did not have a good time. Trying to sell outdated, fifteen-year-old greeting cards sight unseen to florists across the country is not fun. When you did manage to get a sale, the florist would inevitably ship them right back once they got a look at them. Several years back Moderne Card Co. finally met its timely death. In its place sprouted a music venue and restaurant—just like Martyr's. By all accounts this was a decent place with a good crowd. It went out of business almost immediately. So too would Martyr's, I assumed. There was too much bad energy in that place for anyone to ever be able to enjoy themselves in its confines. Surprisingly enough, this has not been the case. You'll find Martyr's a laid-back, decent joint to take in a band, especially if you're into older bands and performers with more "mature" material than your average twentysomething indie rock group. The restaurant serves high-quality bar food—the jerk chicken sandwich is a particular standout—along with Sunday brunch. And Deadhead fans take notice: a very diligent Dead cover band—Dark Star Orchestra—still occasionally plays here, though they no longer have a weekly residency. These guys are the Civil War reenactors of Dead cover bands, covering specific shows with scary accuracy.

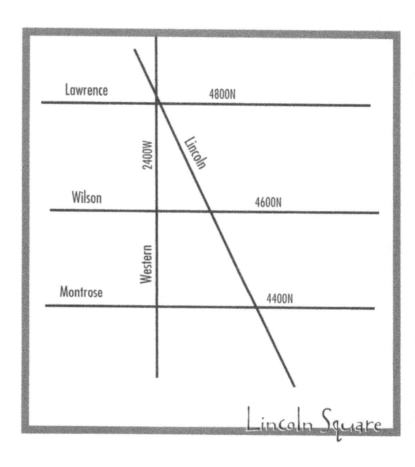

20

LINCOLN SQUARE

Over the course of the '20s, with the extension of the Ravenswood "L" tracks, lands around Lincoln Avenue, once an old Indian path, began to be heavily settled by families moving away from the congestion of the inner city. A large number of them were German, and today they remain the most visible presence in the Lincoln Square area thanks to a small strip of Lincoln at Lawrence that is closed to two-way traffic. Along this strip and south of it are a number of German delis, bakeries, restaurants, and gift shops. Greeks settled in this area as well, especially after the building of both the Eisenhower Expressway and the UIC Circle campus in the '60s chopped away all but a small strip of Greek Town. A couple of Greek restaurants even sit along the one-way German strip, with more further south. Plenty of Koreans and Mexicans live in this area now too, but Lincoln Square still manages to be associated primarily with the German shops clustered near the intersection of Lincoln and Lawrence.

Old Town School of Folk Music

4544 N. Lincoln Avenue 773-728-6000
Hours: Store: Mon–Thu, 10 A.M.–9 P.M.; Fri–Sun, 10 A.M.–
5 P.M.; for performances, call ahead or check paper.

Transplanted a few years back from (you guessed it) Old Town, the Old Town School of Folk Music is a Chicago institution, offering classes and hosting performances by local and national acts. Within its confines you will find a small music shop where you can purchase not just your typical CDs, sheet music, and strings, but guitars and banjos as well. Unfortunately, jugs of corn whisky are not available.

Daily Bar & Grill

4560 N. Lincoln Avenue 773-561-6198
Hours: Mon–Thu, 11:30 A.M.–11 P.M.; Fri, 11:30 A.M.–12 A.M.;
Sat, 10 A.M.–12 A.M.; Sun, 10 A.M.–10 P.M.

"Nouveau" diners became big in Chicago some years back with their overpriced "comfort foods" such as meatloaf and pot roast and such. The Daily Bar & Grill does fit into this niche, but their prices are cheaper than most and the grub is very well done. Or at least better than my mom ever made it. (Note: Mom, I'm only talking about your meatloaf and pot roast and, let's face it, your burgers. Your Italian stuff—the mostaccioli and, especially, the chicken Parmesan, have always been first rate.)

A Secret Closet

4617 N. Lincoln Avenue 773-293-2903
Hours: Mon–Thu, 2 P.M.–7 P.M.; Sat, 11 A.M.–7 P.M.;
Sun, 12 P.M.–5 P.M.

This well-appointed little resale shop has some nice stuff. There isn't a lot of selection of anything in particular, from clothes to housewares, but what they do have is high quality. You can definitely get some fancy-schmancy little knickknacks here, as well as fashionable clothing. As for why this closet should be "secret," well, your guess is as good as mine.

Ravenswood Used Books

4626 N. Lincoln Avenue 773-989-0109
Hours: Wed–Sun, 1 P.M.–6 P.M.; sometimes open on
Mondays, but call first

This little bookshop sports a decent general selection of titles. It's sometimes hard to maneuver in here what with all the books stacked about in the aisles, but this does give the place a rather "charming" clutter, if I may say so. A charming clutter only used bookstores like this are allowed to get away with. (See Bookman's Corner in Lincoln Park for an example of an "uncharmingly" cluttered shop.)

Quake Collectibles

4628 N. Lincoln Avenue 773-878-4628
Hours: Mon, 1 P.M.–6 P.M.; Wed–Fri, 1 P.M.–6 P.M.;
Sat, 12 P.M.–9 P.M.; Sun, 12 P.M.–5 P.M.

This shop carries a wide array of old toys and board games from the '70s and '80s. Haven't played Asteroids since you were a grubby little kid spending your allowance at the local arcade? You can relive those days here—they have a genuine, quarter-guzzling arcade machine in the shop.

Laurie's Planet of Sound

4639 N. Lincoln Avenue 773-271-3569
Hours: Mon–Sat, 10 A.M.–10 P.M.; Sun, 11 A.M.–7 P.M.

This record shop features a little bit of everything. You can find new, used, and import CDs; albums; cassettes; and plenty of quirky videos. This along with sunglasses, T-shirts, a number of books and magazines, and even a few 8-track fricking tapes! A good store.

Chicago Brauhaus

4732 N. Lincoln Avenue 773-784-4444
Hours: Mon, 11 A.M.–2 A.M.; Wed–Sun, 11 A.M.–2 A.M.

A Chicago institution, the Brauhaus serves up big ol'
plates of traditional German food. The best thing
about the place, however, is the nightly live music after
7 P.M. Yes, this is performed by men in lederhosen, who
always get the crowd up and dancing. Neither the food
or drinks are cheap, but you won't find a more casual,
relaxed, upbeat environment, with youngsters and
oldsters alike guzzling steins of beer and whooping it
up. *Ein prosit!*

Delicatessen Meyer

4750 N. Lincoln Avenue 773-561-3377
Hours: Mon–Sat, 9 A.M.–9 P.M.; Sun, 10 A.M.–5 P.M.

This quaint German deli offers a whole lot of stuff.
Imported beers, wines, mustards, and chocolates as
well as fresh cheese and meats. The quality is impecca-
ble, and you'll be surprised at the variety of bratwurst
and liverwurst to choose from. This truly is the land
where the braunschweiger grows!

Barba Yianni Grecian Taverna

4761 N. Lincoln Avenue 773-878-6400
Hours: Sun–Thu, 11 A.M.–12 A.M.; Fri–Sat, 11 A.M.–2 A.M.

If you're a connoisseur of fine Greek food, you probably don't want to eat here. But for my uneducated
palate, the traditional Greek fare they serve up is fine
enough, though I've certainly had much better in
Greek Town. But let's face it, what I'm here for is the
atmosphere. And when I say, "atmosphere," I mean
"the belly dancing on Saturday nights." *Opah!*

Opart Thai House

4658 N. Western Avenue 773-989-8517
Hours: Sun–Thu, 11 A.M.–10 P.M.; Fri–Sat, 11 A.M.–11 P.M.

This little restaurant serves up a limited but very good selection of Thai dishes. I used to work in the area years back, and many a Friday found me and my fellow employees here. The fact that it's BYOB certainly played a role in our decision. We could grab beers at the liquor store one door over and chow down (our boss, I'll have you know, was not only aware of this, but it was always his idea). The food was an equally powerful lure. My favorite entrée is called "Peanut Lover," which, yes, always makes me feel silly when I order it. But get this thing with some chicken or other meat—even tofu, if you prefer—and you're in for a treat. Just keep an eye out for those hot peppers. (Rats—I don't know any appropriate exclamations in Thai to end this with.)

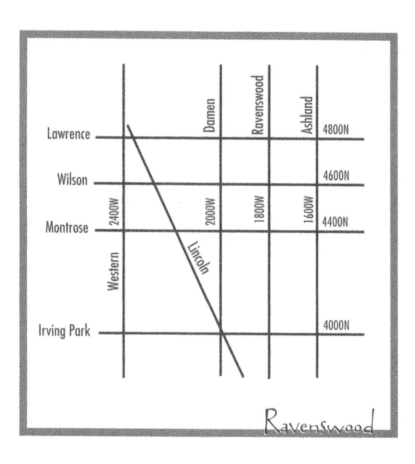

21

RAVENSWOOD

Not a whole lot needs to be said about Ravenswood. Though much more residential than St. Ben, it retains the same basic characteristics. Well-kept apartment buildings and houses line quiet, tree-lined streets. At least, they used to be tree-lined. A few years back Ravenswood was hit by an infestation of the Asian Long-Horned Beetle, and hundreds of trees were cut down. This gives some of Ravenswood's streets an odd look that should persist for some time—older trees interspersed with newly planted saplings. But hey, over a hundred years ago Chicagoans would have no doubt welcomed an infestation of Asian beetles compared to an outbreak of Asiatic cholera, so things really aren't that bad when you think about it.

Beans & Bagels

1812 W. Montrose Avenue 773-769-2000
Hours: Mon–Fri, 7 A.M.–5 P.M.; Sat–Sun,
8:30 A.M.–2:30 P.M.

This coffeeshop is located underneath the Montrose "L" stop and is a convenient place to pop in for a cup of coffee or some grub. They carry quite a few different bagel selections, and though I don't agree with their claim of having the "Best Damn Sandwiches in the City," their sandwiches are certainly tasty and well worth sampling.

Elite Sportscards & Comics

2028 W. Montrose Avenue 773-784-1396
Hours: Mon–Fri, 11 A.M.–5 P.M.; Sat, 11 A.M.–4 P.M.

As the store name suggests, this is the place to go if you're into collecting sports cards. They have quite a collection. Other than the cards, you'll find a small selection of sci-fi memorabilia and toys, as well as current issues of small-press comics.

Club 950

2122 W. Lawrence Avenue 773-878-8241
Hours: Wed-Fri, 7 P.M.–2 A.M.; Sat, 7 P.M.–3 A.M.

Originally located in Lincoln Park, this is one of the more fun places to go if you're looking for an "alternative" dance joint. Club 950 has been up and running for years and has always been a convivial place to hit the floor. Attitude is non-existent here. Their '80s night, "Planet Earth," always packs them in.

22

ANDERSONVILLE

In the late 1860s, the area around Clark and Foster was farmland far removed from the city. In the early 1870s, however, many Swedish families, having done well for themselves in carpentry and various other such skilled trades, moved away from the congestion of the city to build homes there. With the arrival of public transportation to the area in 1908, many more Swedes moved to the region and the neighborhood of Andersonville became firmly established. The exclusively Swedish character of this area only lasted into the '30s; different ethnic groups soon began moving in, culminating in the arrival of many Assyrians in the '70s. Today you'll find Andersonville retains aspects of its Scandinavian heritage primarily in a small number of Swedish bakeries and gift shops—along with the Swedish American Museum. These sit alongside a few Japanese restaurants as well as several Middle Eastern eateries and groceries. These days, though, Andersonville is most closely associated with the gay community. Here you'll find a large gay and lesbian population. But unlike Boys Town to the south, you won't find any outrageous clubs. Most people who live here—both gay and straight—tend more toward

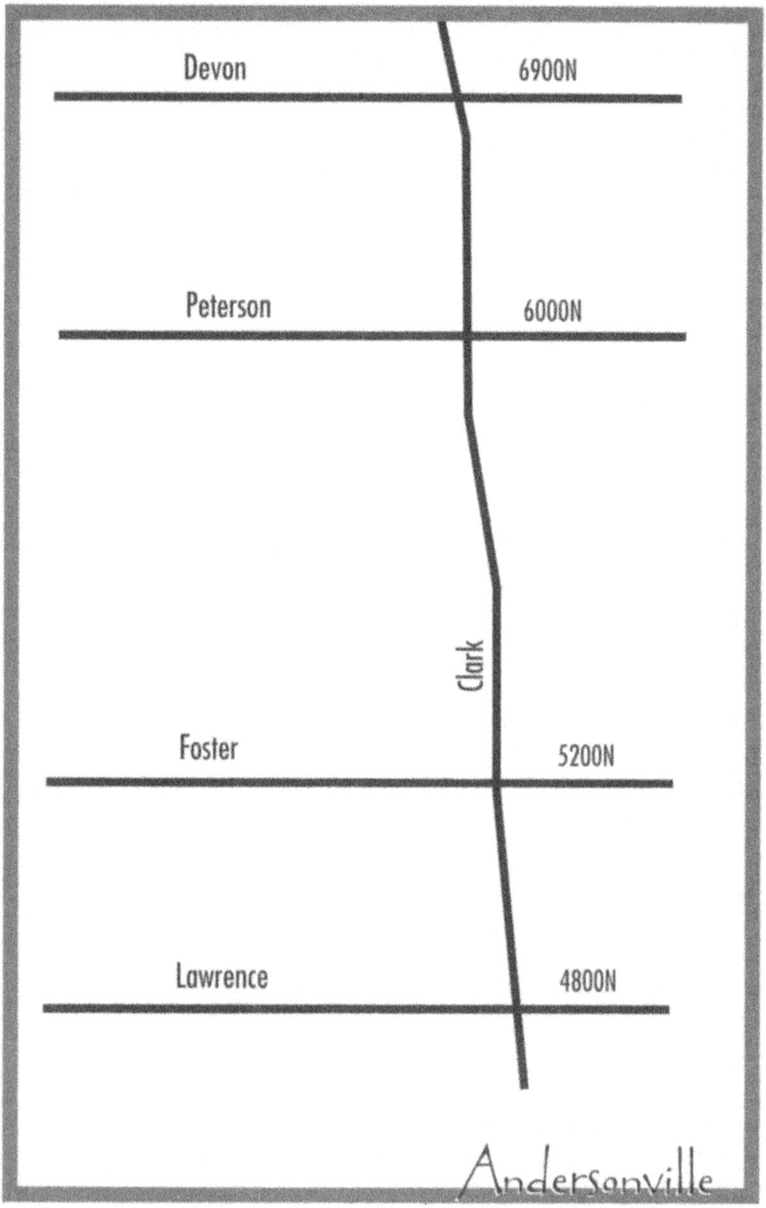

Devon   6900N

Peterson   6000N

Clark

Foster   5200N

Lawrence   4800N

Andersonville

the bohemian and "intellectual" than residents of Boys Town. What you find instead of gay clubs are gay-owned or gay-friendly neighborhood taverns and trendy little restaurants, as well as a number of small theater companies.

Village Discount Outlet

4898 N. Clark Street
Hours: Mon–Fri, 9 A.M.–9 P.M.; Sat, 9 A.M.–6 P.M.;
Sun, 11 A.M.–5 P.M.

Like most of its cousins, this particular Village Discount is large, crowded, muggy, etc. As usual, most of the contents have been picked over pretty thoroughly, but you never know what you might find.

Ann Sather Restaurant

5207 N. Clark Street 773-271-6677
Hours: Mon–Fri, 7 A.M.–3:30 P.M.; Sat–Sun, 7 A.M.–5 P.M.

This is Chicago's premier Swedish restaurant. Sandwich and salad prices are quite reasonable, and though the entrées are a tad expensive you'll find them worth every penny. The Swedish combo will stuff you to the gills with the likes of Swedish meatballs and potatoes. If this was the fare of the Vikings, I'm jealous. They had all this and ale and debauchery too! What a living.

Simon's Tavern

5210 N. Clark Street 773-878-0894
Hours: Open every day, 11 A.M.–2 A.M.

This tavern is no longer owned by the son of the original owner—a Swedish immigrant who opened the place in the '30s. However, Simon's still serves up batches of glogg every Yule season. Believe me, you're not going to find glogg in too many places. And though I'm by no means a glogg expert, I don't imagine you'll find any better this side of Minnesota. A good place to stop by for a beer even in the middle of summer.

The Right Place

5219 N. Clark Street 773-561-7757
Hours: Mon–Thu, 10 A.M.–4 P.M.; Fri–Sat, 11 A.M.–5 P.M.;
Sun, 12 P.M.–4:30 P.M.

Nothing special, this small resale shop offers the usual fare—men and women's clothing, knickknacks, a smattering of furniture, and books and albums. It's worth a quick browse.

Specialty Video & DVD

5225 N. Clark Street 773-878-3434
Hours: Sun–Thu, 10 A.M.–10 P.M.; Fri–Sat, 10 A.M.–11 P.M.

The foreign film section is the pride and joy of Specialty Video, but unfortunately these films are pretty much for rental only. However, they do carry quite a number of independent, offbeat films for sale—both new and used, on VHS and DVD. This is in addition to quality, mainstream films as well. Think of it as your one-stop video shopping joint.

Brown Elephant Resale Shop

5228 N. Clark Street 773-271-9382
Hours: Open every day, 11 A.M.–6 P.M.

Though this is one of the smaller Brown Elephants, you will, as usual, find plenty of good quality stuff here.

Women and Children First Bookstore

5233 N. Clark Street 773-769-9299
Hours: Mon–Tue, 11 A.M.–7 P.M.; Wed–Fri, 11 A.M.–9 P.M.;
Sat, 11 A.M.–7 P.M.; Sun, 11 A.M.–6 P.M.

This is Chicago's only bookshop that specializes in women's studies. Within its confines you'll find extensive sections on feminism, gender politics, and lesbian issues. And the children's section just happens to be one of the best in the city. The store also sponsors readings and talks by various authors and professors.

Svea Restaurant

5236 N. Clark Street 773-275-7738
Hours: Open every day, 7 A.M.–3:45 P.M.

If Ann Sather's appeals to the latent Viking within us all, Svea pulls no punches and boldly declares itself the "Home of the Viking Breakfast!" In this small, kitchen-like space, you can chow down on Swedish pancakes and "Viking"-style French toast (they're stretching it a bit with that one), and other entrées, all of which do indeed come in hearty portions. For lunch you can stuff your gullet with Swedish meatball sandwiches or, for the less-ravenous Norsemen and women among you, herring salads. Definitely worth a visit.

Reza's Restaurant

5255 N. Clark Street 773-561-1898
Hours: Open every day, 11 A.M.–12 A.M.

This place is always packed and convivial—at both lunch and dinner time. After eating here you'll know why. Serving up a plethora of Middle-Eastern food— from lamb and seafood to vegetarian dishes and shishkabob platters, Reza's gives you mountains of food for very reasonable prices. You also get a live piano serenade every night. It don't get much classier than that.

Kopi: A Traveler's Cafe

5317 N. Clark Street 773-989-5674
Hours: Mon–Fri, 8 A.M.–11 P.M.; Sat, 9 A.M.–12 A.M.;
Sun, 10 A.M.–11 P.M.

This cozy, comfortable little coffeehouse bills itself as a traveler's cafe, offering plenty of books and resources on just that topic along with the joe and food. A good place to go and compare notes with fellow travelers. Unfortunately, none of the patrons ever seem all that interested in my extensive travels to exotic Springfield, our mysterious, romantic state capital.

Sunshine Cafe

5449 N. Clark Street 773-334-6214
Hours: Tue–Sun, 12 P.M.–9 P.M.

This is a tiny, friendly, family-owned restaurant serving up homestyle Japanese comfort food like donburi and potato croquets. My wife, who spent her preteen years in Tokyo, swears by this place and often mentions their unagi donburi longingly.

Musician's Network

5505 N. Clark Street 773-728-2929
Hours: Mon, 1 P.M.–7:30 P.M.; Tue–Fri, 11:30 A.M.–
7:30 P.M.; Sat, 10:30–6 P.M.; Sun, 1 P.M.–5 P.M.

This friendly, laid-back shop is a longtime favorite with many local musicians. Not only do they sell new and used instruments and equipment, but they do fast, quality repair work at fair prices.

Salvation Army Thrift Store

5556 N. Clark Street 773-728-8079
Hours: Mon–Sat, 10 A.M.–7 P.M.

Not the most scintillating jewel in the Salvation Army firmament. You'll find this location crowded, hot, and musty—with most of the contents picked over by vintage-store owners and the hipster neighborhood clientele. But—as usual—it's still worth a look.

23

UPTOWN

Uptown is an odd place. I moved to its outskirts back in the mid-'80s at the tender age of nineteen. My apartment was in an area that had more in common with Ravenswood than Uptown really, but the heart of Uptown— Lawrence and Broadway— was only a handful of blocks away. One day I had neither work nor school to occupy my time. Hey, I thought merrily, why not wander down to Lawrence and Broadway— you know, check out the shops and all. Full of enthusiasm and good cheer, I set out. Before an hour had passed I was thoroughly bummed. You see, Uptown had—and still does, though it's been reduced—a large homeless population. The word is that back in the '70s mental institutions could no longer simply lock up their charges and throw away the key. They had to prepare their patients to live and cope in the real world and then release them. Well, whether they were ready or not, a whole batch of them got released in Uptown.

This isn't all of Uptown's problems. Things started going sour even before World War II. By the '60s Uptown was the destination of all those immigrants and new arrivals who could only afford the cheapest of housing. Things got worse

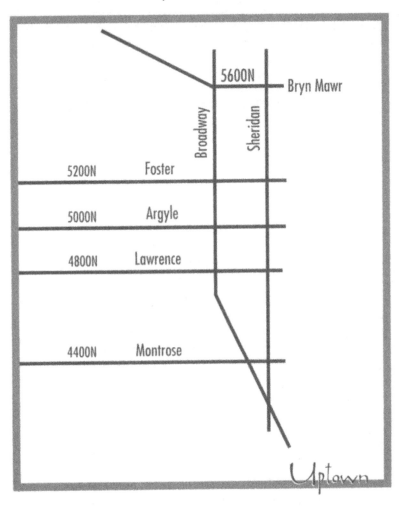

as the government tried to break up the Native American reservation system in an attempt to cure the inhabitants of "Indianness." To do so relocation programs were cooked up—jobs were promised to Native Americans in a variety of cities. Those who took advantage of the program were given a one-way ticket and fifty dollars to reach their destination. And then guess what? There was no job waiting for them after all. Uptown still has a large concentration of Native

Americans, as well as poor white southerners, Vietnamese, Filipinos and other southeast Asians, blacks, and Latinos.

Though parts of Uptown have been gentrified (Sheridan Park is what the Realtors call one of these pockets), much of it is still a bit rough around the edges. One interesting development in the area is the establishment of New Chinatown on Argyle just east of Broadway. After the fall of Saigon, many ethnic Chinese living in Vietnam came to Chicago. And here on Argyle you'll find two whole blocks of shops and restaurants, with an emphasis on Vietnamese food and products.

Basically, Uptown is one of those areas that is definitely worth visiting. But, of course, you have to keep your smarts about you. During the day about the worst you'll have to deal with is an occasional panhandler and the smell of urine wafting out of an alley. Things can get a bit weirder at night since all the bums have gotten even drunker, but plenty of people—suburbanites, natch—mingle about unmolested as a few concert halls are in the neighborhood. So don't be afraid, just be aware. And now I'll stop sounding like your parents.

American Indian Gift Store

1756 W. Wilson Avenue 773-769-1170
Hours: Tue, 12 P.M.–6 P.M.; Thu–Fri, 12 P.M.–6 P.M.,
Sat, 10 A.M.–6 P.M.

This is one of the more unique shops in Chicago. Native American owned and operated, it specializes in pottery, sand paintings, books, CDs and cassettes, Kachina dolls, and a variety of other such Native American made and themed items. You'll find everything from cheap souvenir items to expensive pieces of contemporary art. A very worthwhile place to visit.

Salvation Army Thrift Store

4315 N. Broadway Avenue 773-348-1401
Hours: Mon–Sat, 9 A.M.–9 P.M.

This one offers the usual, unexciting, serviceable fare. You're not apt to find anything too funky or cool here, but then you might get lucky. It does, however, provide a somewhat more rewarding "shopping experience" than the Unique listed below.

Unique Thrift Store

4445 N. Sheridan Road 773-275-8623
Hours: Mon–Fri, 9 A.M.–7 P.M., Sat–Sun, 10 A.M.–5 P.M.

Large, crowded, hot, and picked over, but would you have it any other way? This one happens to have a good-sized parking lot out front so at least it's more convenient than others.

Topper's Recordtown

4619 N. Broadway Avenue 773-878-2032
Hours: Mon–Wed, 10 A.M.–7 P.M.; Thu–Sun, 10 A.M.–6 P.M.

This small, new-and-used music shop specializes primarily in Top 40 soul and R&B. CDs and cassettes only. One cool thing is that most used CDs are only $5.

A–Z Willis Military Surplus

4647 N. Broadway Avenue 773-784-9140
Hours: Mon–Thu, 9:30 A.M.–5:45 P.M.; Fri, 9:30 A.M.–
6:45 P.M.; Sat–Sun, 10 A.M.–5 P.M.

This small surplus shop sells a decent collection of stuff. Pea coats and air force sweaters make up the best of the military items, and a great selection of regular boots, jeans, and sweatshirts rounds out the rest of the merchandise. Prices aren't cheap but are reasonable.

African Wonderland Imports

4713 N. Broadway Avenue 773-334-2293
Hours: Mon–Fri, 10 A.M.–7 P.M.; Sat, 10 A.M.–5 P.M.;
Sun, 11 A.M.–5 P.M.

This shop features a good selection of African clothing as well as carvings, baskets, and various pieces of folk art. They even sell drums—and all at affordable prices.

Equator Club

4715 N. Broadway Avenue 773-728-2411
Hours: Wed–Sun, 9 P.M.–2 A.M.

This unique club has been the only one of its kind in Chicago for a number of years. Inside DJs spin Caribbean and calypso music as well as "Afro-pop" and regular old disco. Covers are a bit up there on weekends but not bad at all during the week.

Green Mill Lounge

4802 N. Broadway Avenue 773-878-5552
Hours: Mon–Fri, 12 P.M.–4 A.M.; Sat, 12 P.M.–5 A.M.;
Sun, 12 P.M.–4 A.M.

A Chicago legend since 1907, the Green Mill is the sort of dark, smoky, den-like place that is perfect for live jazz. Al Capone used to hang out here, and if it's a slow night you might want to ask if you can see the photo scrapbook behind the bar filled with snapshots of that era. Chicago jazz vocalist Kurt Elling and pianist Willie Pickens play here quite a bit along with many other great musicians. Sunday nights The Green Mill plays host to the famous Uptown Poetry Slam, with live music featured throughout the week. Covers can be a bit steep for particular shows but, what the hell, this place is a national treasure.

Shake Rattle and Read

4812 N. Broadway Avenue 773-334-5311
Hours: Mon–Thu, 11 A.M.–6 P.M.; Fri–Sat, 11 A.M.–7 P.M.;
Sun, 11 A.M.–6 P.M.

This is a fun little shop. Primarily a bookstore, it also carries a hodgepodge collection of albums, cassettes, and CDs. The books are mostly mass-market paperbacks, but there are plenty of worthwhile titles mingled among them. One of the highlights of the shop are the many vintage paperbacks from the '50s sporting lurid covers and suggestive titles such as *Topless Kittens* and *Strange Sisters* (I'm sure you can guess just how these sisters manifest their "strangeness"). There are also plenty of current magazines as well as very old back issues, from *Playboy* to *Variety.*

Dr. Wax

1121 W. Berwyn Avenue 773-784-3333
Hours: Mon–Sat, 11 A.M.–9 P.M.; Sun, 12 P.M.–6 P.M.

Originally a longtime resident of Lincoln Park, this Dr. Wax has made the radical move to Uptown. You'll be happy to note, however, that the selection remains outstanding. The CD collection is extensive and eclectic, with good showings in all categories from rock and rap to country. The same holds true for the used vinyl. They also carry a small selection of new vinyl.

Moody's Pub

5910 N. Broadway Avenue 773-275-2696
Hours: Open every day, 11 A.M.–2 A.M.

If it's a burger you're wanting, this is one of the best places to get it. The burger is Moody's speciality and they do it up right. Hell, even if you don't want a burger but simply want to drink a beer in one of the city's finest beer gardens, this is the place for you. Watch out for the squirrels though—they're quite bold. The kitchen's open from 11:30 A.M. to 1 A.M. every day.

NEW CHINATOWN

Cafe Nhu-Hoa

1020 W. Argyle Street 773-878-0618
Hours: Tue–Thu, 10 A.M.–10 P.M.; Fri–Sat, 10 A.M.–
10:30 P.M., Sun, 10 A.M.–10 P.M.

Sporting two elaborate lion statues outside its doors, this pleasant little restaurant serves up Vietnamese and Laotian cuisine. I've only eaten here once and a friend did all the ordering, but everything we sampled—from vegetable dishes to a particularly tasty chicken entrée—was very pleasing to the gullet. The prices are fairly cheap too.

Korea Town / Albany Park

24

KOREA TOWN / ALBANY PARK

Korea Town is spread out through the neighborhood of Albany Park, which is sprawling and relatively nondescript. Heavily Jewish when it was first settled in the early 1900s, Albany Park remained that way up until after World War II. By the early '70s most of the Jewish families had moved to the suburbs and urban decay was setting in. Then the Koreans arrived. Soon scores of storefronts were emblazoned with Korean logos. This upset many of the homeowners in the area, mostly Greek, Polish, and Latino, who heavily outnumbered the Koreans actually living in the vicinity. Harmony has been found these days, however, and the neighborhood has shed its somewhat tattered image to become a respectable area, though I must say traffic on one of the main drags—Lawrence Avenue—can get atrocious. Amid the Greek and Middle Eastern establishments you'll find dozens of Korean restaurants, groceries, and shops. From stores selling trinkets to auto repair garages, the variety is impressive if not exactly glamorous.

Korea Restaurant

2659 W. Lawrence Avenue 773-878-2095
Hours: Open 24 hours

This imaginatively named restaurant is exactly what it purports to be: a Korean restaurant. It's nothing fancy and a bit too brightly lit if you wander in here during the wee hours after a long bender, but the prices are reasonable and you get plenty of appetizers and decent-sized portions. The kalbee is particularly good.

Village Discount Outlet

3301 Lawrence Avenue
Hours: Mon–Fri, 9 A.M.–9 P.M.; Sat, 9 A.M.–6 P.M.;
Sun, 11 A.M.–5 P.M.

I'm sure you know the score by now. This one is large and cluttered, but no less crowded or slightly moldy smelling. You'll have a somewhat better chance of finding cool knickknacks at this one, but I guarantee nothing.

Chicago's Underground Music

3320 W. Lawrence Avenue 773-267-6140
Hours: Mon–Sat, 10 A.M.–8:30 P.M.; Sun, 10 A.M.–6 P.M.

The name of this music store is definitely a misnomer, since the majority of their stock is very radio friendly. The emphasis is on rap and R&B, though they have a pretty wide-ranging general selection. You can also pick up some sunglasses and a few toys and novelty items with that "underground rock 'n' roll" flair.

Garden Buffet

5347 Lincoln Avenue 773-728-1249
Hours: Mon–Fri, 11:30 A.M.–11 P.M.; Sat, 12 P.M.–11 P.M.

This spacious restaurant features a huge, tasty buffet, with a wide variety of vegetable and meat dishes, sushi, and raw meats for "personal" barbecuing. The only problem is that it can get a bit expensive if you do indeed want to make use of the little barbecue pit at

the table. Dinners can set you back $17 a person.
However, if you go in there at lunchtime and don't use
the barbecue, you're only looking at about a measly $8
a person. This is well worth it as you'll have no need to
eat for the next two days. Get yourself a big ol' bottle of
Obee beer as well.

New Outdoor Cafe

3257 W. Bryn Mawr Avenue 773-539-6078
Hours: Open every day, 1 P.M.–12 A.M.

This cafe does not have outdoor seating, but it's set up
like it's outdoors. The flooring is like a backyard rock
garden, with circular stepping stones ushering you up
to the counter. A rather interesting concept, I must say.
Of course if they actually had outdoor seating it would
be better, but you have to give this place credit for
working with what it's got. Here you can get the usual
joe, along with sweets, smoothies, and those bubble
teas the kids are drinking these days. Perhaps I'm
showing my age, but I must admit I find those things
somewhat disturbing. One of these days someone's
going to choke on one of those tapioca balls, and no
one will find that very hip, will they?

The Abbey Pub

3420 W. Grace Street 773-478-4408
Hours: Restaurant: Tue–Fri, 2 P.M.–10 P.M.; Sat–Sun,
9 A.M.–10 P.M.; Concert Room: Sun–Thu, 8 P.M.–2 A.M.;
Fri, 9 P.M.–2 A.M.; Sat, 9 P.M.–3 A.M.

The Abbey has been around for years, but up until
fairly recently it was considered an Irish pub, with
most of the acts that played here heavily inclined
toward traditional Irish music. These days a wide variety of acts play here, from rock and punk to country
and blues. It's a very comfortable place to see a band,
as you can usually find a seat if you're so inclined—
especially in the balcony that rings the main floor. You
can also gobble down a traditional Irish breakfast on

Saturdays and Sundays, as well as catch any number of international sporting events. Wonder what's happening with your favorite rugby team? This is one of the few bars in the city where you can find out.

Adam's Apple

6229 N. California Avenue 773-465-9777
Hours: Open every day, 1 P.M.–7 P.M.

This small, ancient head shop has been around since the '60s. Outside of the good collection of bowls and bongs—oops, I mean cigarette coolers—you can find plenty of nuttily sloganed T-shirts and those overly baggy jeans the kids wear.

25

DEVON AVENUE

Just west of Western Avenue, Devon becomes one of the city's most interesting streets. Within the span of only a few blocks you'll find a polyglot of cultures. Jewish bookstores and delis; Indian restaurants, electronic stores, and sari shops; Russian bookstores; Pakistani eateries; the Croatian Cultural Center—all call this strip home. You can literally walk for a number of blocks and not hear a word of English. From what I understand, Indians from all over the Midwest make shopping pilgrimages here, and many recent immigrants from the various nationalities flock here both to live and shop. If nothing else, you should at least take a drive through.

Salvation Army Thrift Store

2151 W. Devon Avenue 773-262-3645
Hours: Mon–Fri, 10 A.M.–7:45 P.M.;
Sat, 10 A.M.–5:45 P.M.

This is a good-sized Salvation Army store, and it even has a parking lot. The predominant item here is clothing, with rack upon rack of standard shirts, pants, dresses, and jeans for every member of the family. The emphasis really is on family, for you won't find anything particularly funky here, just regular old clothes. A decent amount of furniture and housewares is available also, but these fit the same billing as the clothes.

Bundoo Khan Restaurant

2501 W. Devon Avenue 773-743-6800
Hours: Mon–Fri, 11 A.M.–1 P.M.; Sat, 11 A.M.–12 A.M.;
Sun, 12 P.M.–10 P.M.

This low-key Pakistani restaurant is quite a deal, serving up lunch buffets for $6.99 and dinner buffets for only a dollar more. There's plenty to choose from for both the carnivore and the vegetarian, and though I'm not too familiar with Pakistani food, I did particularly relish the chicken dish. I think it was called Chicken Tikka, or perhaps Tikka chicken. Does that a ring a bell

at all? Whatever it's called, it sure was good. This is a
great place to fill up the innards on the cheap.

Gandhi India Restaurant

2601 W. Devon Avenue 773-761-8714
Hours: Sun–Thu, 11:30 A.M.–3:30 P.M. and 5 P.M.–10 P.M.;
Fri-Sat, 11:30 A.M.–3:30 P.M. and 5 P.M.–11 P.M.

In this attractive, casual restaurant, you can get some
very good curries and Tandoori chicken. Plenty of
seafood, lamb, and vegetarian dishes are also available
at decent, reasonable prices. The Indian beer is good,
but they also have a whole slew of "exotic" drinks you
might want to try.

Russian American Book Store

2746 W. Devon Avenue 773-761-3233
Hours: Open every day, 10 A.M.–7 P.M.

Here you'll find a large collection of books, magazines,
and newspapers, along with a variety of knickknacks,
dolls, and—to use a phrase those French-speaking
Czarist oppressors of old would've employed—objets
d'art. Unfortunately for those of us who have no com-
prehension of Russian, most of the reading material is
indeed in that language. However, the charming old
proprietor will be more than happy to direct you to the
small collection of English-language books in stock.
And not only will he suggest a few selections, he'll tell
you a few tales of the old country as well. An interesting little shop.

New York Kosher Sausage Corporation

2900 W. Devon Avenue 773-338-3354
Hours: Sun, 8 A.M.–6 P.M.; Mon–Wed, 8 A.M.–7 P.M.;
Thu, 8 A.M.–9 P.M.; Fri, 8 A.M.–6 P.M.

Don't let the foreboding, official-sounding name fool
you—this is nothing but a small, neighborhood grocery. The meat counter in the back is what sets it apart
from other such shops. Here you can get decent, reasonably priced, no-frills sandwiches. Pastrami and

corned beef are the specialties of course, but if you've got a hankering for a plain old baloney sandwich, you can indulge that urge here as well.

26
ROGERS PARK

The last stop before the border of Evanston, Rogers Park is a widely varied neighborhood. Originally home to middle-class Swedes and Irish, it was incorporated into Chicago in 1893. An influx of Orthodox Jewish families began arriving in the '20s. By the '60s, the western part of the neighborhood was primarily Jewish, with a very strong presence remaining to this day. To the east things are different—and a little bit shady, though not to the degree they were over ten years ago, when a late-night stroll home from the Morse "L" could occasionally find the air filled with a heavy dose of what can only be called "bad vibes." East Rogers Park is very diverse, its population made up of every ethnic and income group you can think of. Near the lake are expensive homes and apartments. Not far away are low-income housing and even projects. I lived in Rogers Park back in 1990, in a building full of other white, college-age residents like me. Next door was a halfway home for the mentally ill. Across the street was a low-income apartment building. The rest of the block was filled with middle-class, mostly white homeowners—a smattering of minority families among them. This is a pretty fair indication of

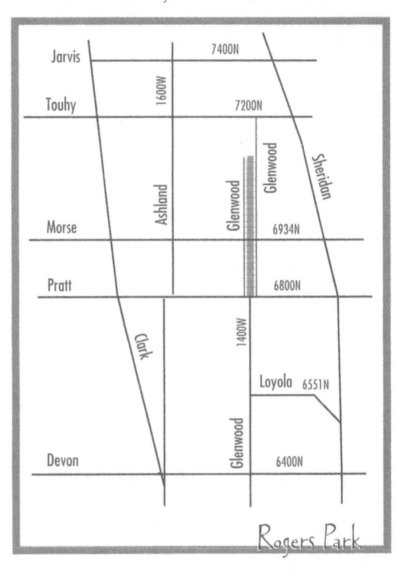

how the neighborhood as a whole is comprised, though these days—like most areas of the North Side—things are gentrifying, with property values going up and the "lower classes" being shunted aside. There are also plenty of college students roaming around, as Loyola University is in the vicinity. A large hippie community used to exist here at one time, and even vestiges of that can be found in the neighborhood. Though a bit out of the way, Rogers Park is definitely one of the more unique areas of the city. And surprisingly enough, its many small, unheralded beaches are among some of the nicest in the city.

Rocket 69

5959 N. Kenmore Avenue, #100 773-293-2294
Hours: Mon–Sat, 10 A.M.–10 P.M.; Sun, 11 A.M.–8 P.M.

This little combination head shop/hipster boutique has been around forever, only it used to sit right near the Clark-Belmont intersection. Inside you'll find a few bongs and bowls along with "alternative" greeting cards, candles, and incense, and various Hindu statuettes and such. Back in the old days us suburban gadabouts always made sure to include this place on our evening's itinerary. We were damn glad to have it too. Unlike you spoiled youngsters, we didn't have an endless succession of cool shops to visit.

The Armadillo's Pillow

6753 N. Sheridan Road 773-761-2558
Hours: Open every day, 12 P.M.–8 P.M.

This is a small, attractive used bookstore. The decor will make you think you stepped into a beautiful, hippie acid fantasy. No real specialization, but a decent enough general selection of both fiction and nonfiction.

Leona's Restaurant

6935 N. Sheridan Road 773-764-5757
Hours: Mon–Thu, 11:30 A.M.–11 P.M.; Fri–Sat, 11:30 A.M.–12:30 A.M.; Sun, 10:30 A.M.–10:30 P.M.

As you're no doubt already aware, this small, family-owned chain of restaurants serves up what I consider to be Chicago's best thin-crust pizza. Dining in is always a casual, pleasant experience. Besides the pizza you can get full dinners—pasta to seafood—as well as an excellent selection of specialty sandwiches.

Unan Imports

6971 N. Sheridan Road 773-274-4022
Hours: Mon–Sat, 11 A.M.–7 P.M.; Sun, sometimes 1 P.M.–5 P.M.,
sometimes closed

This shop offers a large collection of African carvings, jewelry, and crafts. The prices are quite reasonable, and there are a number of very beautiful pieces here. A unique little place.

Ennui Cafe

6981 N. Sheridan Road 773-973-2233
Hours: Sun–Thu, 7:30 A.M.–11 P.M.; Fri–Sat,
7:30 A.M.–1 A.M.

Bright, airy, and homey, this pleasant cafe allows you plenty of space in which to spread out. Fresh juice, bagels, and assorted pastries and sandwiches are offered along with the java. And let me tell you—they make a mean tiramisu. Outside seating is available during the warmer months.

No Exit Cafe

6970 N. Glenwood Avenue 773-743-3355
Hours: Varies; call ahead for performance schedule

Not only is No Exit one of the best cafes in the city, but it is a Chicago institution, having been around for years. A funky, cluttered, comfortable little place, its hippie origins are still visible. There are performances practically every night, from music to improv theater and poetry readings. A very friendly, relaxing place.

Heartland Cafe

7000 N. Glenwood Avenue 773-465-8005
Hours: Mon–Fri, 7 A.M.–2 A.M.; Sat, 8 A.M.–3 A.M.;
Sun, 8 A.M.–2 A.M.

Though some might disagree with labeling this place a Chicago institution, they definitely can't deny its status as a Rogers Park institution. A combination cafe/general store/bar/restaurant/club, the Heartland "compound" features an extensive, reasonably priced, vegetarian-friendly menu; a good selection of beer; and nightly music. The acts range from jazz to world beat to '70s R&B cover bands. A very friendly place, it's the sort of joint to hit when you're tired of feeling cynical and jaded. And that's why you should never come here with my old buddy Mikey, who tends to personify those traits. The only time I've ever seen anyone get angry at this bastion of good vibes was because of him. While chatting with a nice, older hippie woman, he uttered a snort of contempt when she mentioned with pride that her father had played for the NBC Orchestra. "That's just a TV orchestra," he muttered. Whoo boy, when a hippie gets violent it's never pretty.

Turtle Island Books

7001 N. Glenwood Avenue 773-465-7212
Hours: Tue–Sat, 11 A.M.–7 P.M.; Sun, 12 P.M.–6 P.M.

This attractive, new-and-used bookstore specializes in new-age spirituality. You can also buy incense, oils, and crystals here as well as get a tarot reading. And say hello to the smart-ass parakeet in the corner.

The Harvest

1447 W. Jarvis Avenue 773-761-4600
Hours: Tue–Fri, 2 P.M.–7 P.M.; Sat, 12 P.M.–7 P.M.

This elegantly cluttered resale shop ("resale" sounds a bit crude in this case) is chock-full of very nice stuff. From knickknacks and assorted bric-a-brac to housewares and a bit of furnishings, this is a great place to browse about.

Open Brain Books

1441 W. Jarvis Avenue
Hours: Mon–Fri, 4:30 P.M.–12 A.M.; Sat–Sun, 12 P.M.–12 A.M.

This tiny shop features a decent if unremarkable collection of titles. They have a number of different subjects, but not a whole lot of stock in any particular area. It is, however, a rather somnambulant little place, and browsing here is actually quite relaxing. That is if you're the lone patron. If someone else enters, it gets quite crowded, especially considering all the floor space the handsome dog sleeping by the front door takes up.

27

GREEK TOWN

This is only a tiny remnant of the original Greek Town that began taking form in the late 1890s. The establishment of the Eisenhower Expressway and the UIC campus pared it down to what it is today—essentially just a three-block strip of Halsted from Adams on the north to Jackson on the south. Greek Town used to be an informal sort of place in which to hang out. I remember going there with my sisters for Easter when I was eighteen. I wanted to order wine with my dinner but decided against it due to the fact that I was, of course, underage. When I ordered a Coke, the waiter frowned distastefully and told me I would have wine instead. I didn't argue with him. In 1996, Chicago hosted the Democratic National Convention at the United Center, and since Greek Town isn't far from there, it was spruced up for the convention. You'll now find a few Athens-like columns sprouting up on a couple of corners. But they didn't stop there. Some of the restaurants disappeared, and the ones remaining got major facelifts. They've become upscale. Gone are the days when you could feel comfortable stumbling into one of these joints dressed in a T-shirt and a pair of shorts and dine alongside nattily attired businessmen and their wives. Yet the food in these places is still excellent, and I can certainly force myself to don more presentable clothing in order to have a go at it. But if you're underage and ask for a bottle of wine these days, expect to get carded.

Christian Industrial League Resale Shop

112 S. Halsted Street 312-421-2420
Hours: Tue–Sat, 9 A.M.–4:30 P.M.

This is your basic resale shop. A smattering of very normal clothes and a large selection of dishes and drinking glasses are about all you're gonna get here.

Athenian Candle Company

300 S. Halsted Street 312-332-6988
Hours: Mon–Tue, 9:30 A.M.–6 P.M.; Thu–Fri, 9:30 A.M.–
6 P.M.; Sat, 9:30 A.M.–5 P.M.

This candle shop is the real thing—they make them right in the back room. Here you can buy candles for whatever you desire—for wealth, love, or general happiness. This is primarily a religious shop—but not in a Christian or Pagan or Greek Orthodox or New Age or any other sort of easily identifiable way. Along with the multitude of candles are oils and incenses, icons, prayer and blessing cards, and various other spiritual doodads. Prices range from expensive to ridiculously cheap. You can actually buy candles as long as your arm for six bucks. And these aren't crappy ones that immediately sputter and die either. A very interesting place.

Zorba's

301 S. Halsted Street 312-454-0784
Hours: Open 24 hours

My favorite place for gyros, Zorba's still retains its somewhat gritty atmosphere. Here you'll find a large selection of food, from the aforementioned gyros to full-on Greek dinners to burgers and hot dogs. Zorba's comes in most handy for carry-out after 2:00 A.M. when you're looking to sop up the beer with some meat and grease. During more respectable hours when it's not so crowded, however, you can easily get a table or hang out with the old timers at the bar in back.

The Parthenon Restaurant

314 S. Halsted Street 312-726-2407
Hours: Open every day, 11 A.M.–1 A.M.

My favorite Greek Town restaurant, the Parthenon has been remodeled and looks quite swank. As I mentioned earlier, most of these restaurants have classed up their images and atmosphere in the last few years.

Dining here is still casual, only now I wear a decent shirt and pair of jeans and try to be reasonably sober. The food is outstanding—especially the lamb dishes. And the potatoes, of course. The Greeks really have a way with potatoes, don't they? In addition you'll find a whole slew of items on the menu, from seafood to steaks to broiled quail. Prices aren't cheap, but they're not so steep that you can't order a bottle of wine with your meal. And the food is definitely worth the dent in your wallet.

28

LITTLE ITALY

Just like Greek Town, this is only a small remnant of the original Little Italy, though the Italians managed to retain a bit more territory than the Greeks. This area grew from a rough ghetto populated mostly by immigrants from southern Italy into a respectable, middle-class neighborhood full of well-kept houses and yards. So imagine the surprise of the residents when they discovered most of the neighborhood was to be stomped out to make way for the University of Illinois Circle Campus. Mayor Richard J. Daley the Elder refused to hear their pleas and sent them packing back in the early '60s.

Little Italy today is indeed populated by Italians—they don't just run the delis, restaurants, and shops along Taylor Street. Since this is a very sedate, safe neighborhood, it might come as a surprise that projects sit right smack in the middle of it. Apparently these aren't a source of trouble to the neighborhood at all. Of course this leads to jokes about the mob policing the streets, but I wouldn't put much stock in them. My mother's side of the family is as Italian as they come—my grandparents grew up in the general area—and the closest mob connection is the close proximity of Al Capone's grave to that of my great-grandmother's (then again, I've recently learned that my great-grandfather was heavily involved in "union work" and that two of his cousins were gunned down in mob hits back in the late '20s, so who knows?). Chicago Italians, I might add, are very sensitive about being compared to mobsters. You should have heard the hullabaloo they raised in protest over the touristy Al Capone "museum" that lived a short life in River North back in the mid-1990s.

Al's #1 Italian Beef

1079 W. Taylor Street 312-226-4017
Hours: Open every day, 9 A.M.–1 A.M.

A Chicago institution, Al's has been serving up Italian beef for quite some time. Prices have gone up over the years, but for only a few bucks you can still get a heaping, weighty hulk of an Italian beef sandwich that will fill you up good and proper. They also serve your typical burgers and such, but the Italian beef is definitely the must-try.

Mario's Lemonade Stand

W. Taylor Street in the middle of the block between
Aberdeen and Carpenter
Hours: Open every day May to October, 10 A.M.–10 P.M.

Another Chicago—not just a Taylor Street—institution.
Mario's serves up the best Italian ice you're ever apt to
have the pleasure of eating, chock-full of real fruit.
You'll always find lines of people, but you can order
the stuff by the gallon and keep it in your own freezer
if you're so inclined. No summer is complete without
at least one pilgrimage to Mario's.

Conte di Savoia

1438 W. Taylor Street 312-666-3471
Hours: Mon–Sat, 9 A.M.–7 P.M.; Sun, 9 A.M.–4 P.M.

This deli has been around since the late 1940s and
even has a number of old-timers sitting out in front
during the warmer months. Here you can get a large
selection of tasty, cheap Italian sandwiches, as well as
take-out "party" trays of lasagna and chicken parmi-
giano and such. They also carry a wide assortment of
wine.

The Rosebud

1500 W. Taylor Street 312-942-1117
Hours: Mon–Thu, 11 A.M.–9 P.M.; Fri, 11 A.M.–11:30 P.M.;
Sat, 5 P.M.–11:30 P.M.; Sun, 4 P.M.–10 P.M.

Though you can't go wrong at any of the restaurants
on Taylor Street, the Rosebud is is a little less formal
than the others. In fact, they even have "formal" and
"informal" dining areas. You don't get specialized,
regional Italian cooking here, just your simple Italian
classics. It will set you back a bit financially, but the
food is well worth it.

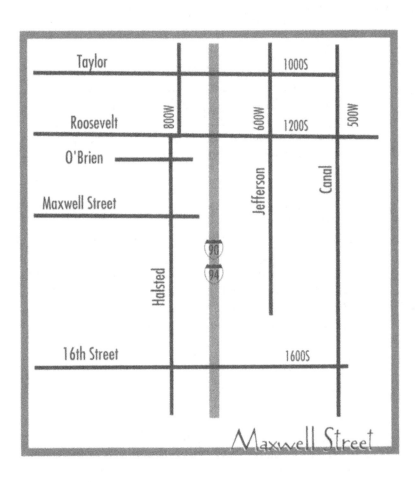

Maxwell Street

29

MAXWELL STREET

M axwell Street is the most well-known thoroughfare in a neighborhood that used to be called Jew Town. Back around the turn of the century, the area was an intensely overcrowded ghetto packed with thousands of Jewish Eastern European immigrants. Jewish shops and eateries dominated the neighborhood, along with hundreds of vendors selling fruits, vegetables, knives, trinkets, and other such merchandise from hand-pulled carts. From this emerged the outdoor Maxwell Street Market. In only a decade, many Jewish families had saved enough money to move, yet most merchants retained their shops in the area. The neighborhood then became host to a large concentration of African Americans, and it was here that the Chicago blues sound became defined, with bands jamming at the market.

These days the Maxwell Street Market has been removed a mile east to Canal Street. Good ol' UIC wanted the land for parking lots. Up until recently, the two-block stretch of Halsted between Roosevelt and Maxwell played host to a slew of clothing stores operated primarily by Arabic merchants. These shops catered to the residents of nearby projects, selling everything from sportswear to fancy duds. Now, however, that's all gone. In fact, any subsequent editions of this book will have to refer to this area as "University Village." Yep, UIC has laid claim to the entire area, and expensive new condos are popping up by the minute to house its faculty and students. Considering the area long had a shabby, neglected, almost third-world appearance, it's hard to complain about the improvements, but did they have to make it look like some sort of suburban townhouse development? Ah well, at least Jim's—the Polish sausage joint listed below—still exists, only it was relocated toward the expressway, where the new residents of "University Village" hope its grease-and-onion-laden emissions waft toward the projects to the east rather than their overpriced condos.

Maxwell Street Market

Canal Street between Taylor and Sixteenth Streets
Hours: Every Sunday rain or shine from (officially)
7 A.M.–3 P.M.

Though a pale copy of the original Maxwell Street Market a mile to the west, this is still a colorful place to be on Sundays. You still have musicians jamming and plenty of food stalls grilling up goodies. And the range of merchandise is still impressive. Here you can barter for anything from tools and tires to fruits and vegetables, clothing and stereo equipment, books and mouthwash. The Maxwell Street Market is a living bit of Chicago history—bastardized history at this point, but history all the same.

Manny's Coffee Shop & Deli

1141 S. Jefferson Street 312-939-2855
Hours: Mon–Sat, 5 A.M.–4 P.M.

In business since 1942, Manny's is an old-style Jewish cafeteria that's hardly changed since the day it opened. Always hopping with customers, Manny's serves up everything from bacon and eggs to Salisbury steaks and Hungarian goulash. Its specialty, however, is its corned beef sandwiches. Though you'll find Manny's surprisingly expensive, you won't argue with the quality. A corned beef sandwich will set you back seven smackers, but the thing is piled with meat and comes with the world's tastiest potato pancake and pickle. The potato pancake itself is almost worth the price.

White Palace Grill

🍴 *1159 S. Canal Street 312-939-7167*
Hours: Open 24 hours

Though recently remodeled, this little greasy spoon diner, built in 1939, has retained its original appearance. A classic eggs and hash, burger and dog joint, you'll find this place gets particularly busy during the breakfast hours.

Jim's

🍴 *700 W. O'Brien Street 312-733-7820*
Hours: Open 24 hours

Though no longer located at the corner of Halsted and Maxwell, it still doesn't get any more quintessentially Chicago than Jim's. At this ratty little hot dog stand you'll find the best Polish sausage sandwich anywhere. This is not simply a fat hot dog on a bun, but a genuine bit of red, mottled, angry sausage. After simmering, this bad boy is charred, heaped with fried onions, and served on a bun with mustard. Two bucks and it's yours. But be careful, after a night of heavy drinking—when it goes down the best—this magnificent Polish tends to take its revenge. Make sure you're near comfortable bathroom facilities.

30

PILSEN

Pilsen, like the Maxwell Street area, has also been the subject of controversy considering it too has been affected both by UIC's expansion and the city's plan for urban renewal. Pilsen was out of the Great Fire's path in 1871, and consequently a good portion of its buildings are more than 130 years old. Many of them are not in great shape, and as Pilsen serves as the arrival point for Mexican immigrants, the area is not exactly bursting with riches. In the old days Germans and Irish originally settled here and worked in the many nearby factories, but after the fire the area became predominantly Czech— or Bohemian, we should say, as Czechoslovakia didn't actually come into existence until after World War I. The neighborhood remained "respectable" up until the end of World War II, but then began declining as most of the Czech families left for the suburbs. Mexican immigrants began taking advantage of the cheap rents, and that process has continued to this day. So no, the overall economic status of Pilsen hasn't improved much over the decades, yet it's hardly "blighted" as the city contends. The western part of Pilsen is a loud, colorful place during the spring and summer, with music leaking out

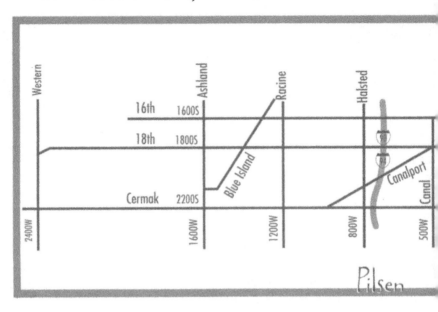

onto the streets from the open doors of the shops and the bells of the street vendors continually ringing. Large murals are also splashed across a number of buildings.

To the east, things are different. Along Halsted a very white "artists" colony has sprung up over the years, a colony of which I myself used to be a resident. As this influx of whites has grown stronger recently, Mexican homeowners have become worried that their property taxes will soon grow to the point that a number of them will no longer be able to afford to remain in the area. Realistically, that is probably exactly what will happen. As every square foot of the North Side in close proximity to the Loop gentrifies, more whites— both professionals as well as students and artists— are moving into the areas directly south of the Loop, where the process is being repeated. Though I only rented in Pilsen, I did feel a bit guilty about being part of this wave. But then again, it's not like the Mexicans have been here forever— only since the '50s really, and as you've probably realized by now in reading this book, Chicago neighborhoods are always changing. Whether this is for better or worse, who's to say?

Lawrence's Fisheries

2120 S. Canal Street 312-225-2113
Hours: Open 24 hours

For my money, this is the best place to get fried shrimp
in the city, not to mention catfish, seafood gumbo,
scallops, frog legs, etc. Lawrence's is loud, crowded,
and right off the river, but if you've got a hankering for
some greasy fried seafood this is the place to go. There
are tables but this is primarily a take-out joint. A great
place to hit after a night of drinking.

Chela Joe's Cafe

1733 S. Halsted Street 312-850-9360
Hours: Mon-Thu, 7 A.M.–10 P.M.; Sat, 10 A.M.–12 A.M.;
Sun, 10 A.M.–3 P.M.

This coffee shop is part of the changing face of Pilsen.
Once a Mexican-owned hardware store, it became Bic's
Hardware Cafe, catering to the predominantly white
artist crowd who live along this strip. In its present
incarnation as Chela Joe's, you'll find it remains the
same pleasant, laid-back, unpretentious little joint that
it was as Bic's, with pretty much the same clientele. On
the second and last Friday of each month they host an
open mike night, where performers indulge in everything from poetry to puppetry.

Cuernavaca Restaurant

1158 W. Eighteenth Street 312-829-1147
Hours: Open every day, 10 A.M.–12 A.M.

This is a very attractive Mexican restaurant, with high
ceilings and a very impressive-looking bar. Although
it's much more than a taqueria, you can nonetheless
order a plain old burrito for cheap; full-on dinners,
however, are more their thing. These tend to be expensive, but the quality is first rate. There's actually a parking lot out front, making this one of the more
convenient places to eat in Pilsen.

Cafe Jumping Bean

1439 W. Eighteenth Street 312-455-0019
Hours: Mon–Fri, 7:00 A.M.–10 P.M.; Sat, 9 A.M.–8 P.M.;
Sun, 11 A.M.–6 P.M.

This colorful cafe serves as a meeting place for many of Pilsen's artists and activists. Pilsen's Mexican artists and activists, that is, rather than a white beachhead in the midst of the Mexican-owned groceries and shops. Here along with the coffee you can get some decent sandwiches and soup.

Nuevo Leon Restaurant

1515 W. Eighteenth Street 312-421-1517
Hours: Sun–Thu, 7 A.M.–12 A.M.; Fri–Sat, 7 A.M.–4 A.M.

Pilsen's best-known eatery, Nuevo Leon is an upscale taqueria serving everything from taco plates to huge carne asada and guisado de puerco platters. Prices are reasonable and the atmosphere is very casual.

Salvation Army Thrift Store

2024 S. Western Avenue 773-254-1127
Hours: Mon–Sat, 9 A.M.–9 P.M.

This one is hotter and mustier than most, with an unspectacular array of clothes, furniture, and assorted bric-a-brac. If you're in the area you might as well give it a look-see, but I wouldn't plan a day trip around it.

31

CHINATOWN

Chinatown sprang up just after the turn of the century. Pushed south by rising rents as well as racism, most Chinese were forced to settle in their present location in what was then the fringes of the red-light district—a neighborhood they certainly wouldn't have chosen on their own. Though the red-light district faded, Chinatown didn't begin to flourish until after World War II. Why, you ask? Well, it wasn't until 1943 that our ever-so-enlightened Congress repealed the Exclusion Act, which since 1882 had kept Chinese and other Asians from immigrating to the U.S. It took the Japanese invasion of China and Southeast Asia to change Anglo sympathies. After the war a steady stream of immigrants began arriving, and with the advent of the Communist revolution in China, many of these immigrants were now skilled, educated, and well-to-do. By the '60s Chinatown was flourishing, filled with restaurants, shops, and laundries. These days an outdoor mall—Chinatown Square—has been added, and a nice little park along the river has been built. You'll also find new condos sprouting up in every available square foot of space, as Chinese immigrants continue to pour into the city. Though

Chinatown proper isn't very large in square blocks, there are more than enough restaurants, groceries, and gift shops along Wentworth Avenue and in the Square to fill up your innards and drain your wallet.

Penang

2201 S. Wentworth Avenue 312-326-6888
Hours: Open every day, 11 A.M.–1 A.M.

> This is a fairly recent addition to Chinatown, and as a sleekly designed, upscale establishment, it's a rarity in the area. It's also rare in that it serves Malaysian cuisine, but since there's no "Malaytown" in Chicago, why not? This place offers up an excellent array of dishes, from noodle soups and fried noodles to curries and various meat, seafood, and vegetable concoctions. It's not exactly dirt cheap, but outside of a few seafood entrées, the prices are very reasonable.

Won Kow Restaurant

2237 S. Wentworth Avenue 312-842-7500
Hours: Sun–Thu, 9 A.M.–11 P.M.; Fri–Sat, 9 A.M.–12 A.M.

Around since 1927, this is the oldest restaurant in Chinatown, and it does a brisk business no matter what the time of year or day of the week. From beef to pork to chicken to seafood or even tofu, I've never had anything but a very tasty meal here. Prices are reasonable, and their spicy dishes are perfect. Plus, if you can read Chinese or you bring someone along with you who can, whoo boy, you can order from the Chinese menu as opposed to the "ghost people" menu, which will net you some incredible food. This is the sort of place that's nice enough to bring your suburban parents to, but laid-back enough to show up in jeans or shorts. They also serve Dim Sum daily.

Chiu Quon Bakery

2242 S. Wentworth Avenue 312-225-6608
Hours: Open every day, 7 A.M.–9 P.M.

This little bakery has a great selection of bean and meat pastries as well as sweets for ridiculously cheap prices. You can order a sackful of stuff for only five bucks.

China Restaurant

2253 S. Wentworth Avenue 312-225-2600
Hours: Mon–Thu, 4 P.M.–2 A.M.; Fri–Sat, 4 P.M.–3 A.M.;
Sun, 2 P.M.–2 A.M.

This dim, sedate little place first attracted me due to the tropical drinks advertised on their sign. And yes, the Dr. Fong drink may indeed be the cure for what ails you as the menu proclaims, but I'm a little more partial to the Mongolian beef. They cook this stuff up right. As far as their other selections go, you probably won't achieve gastronomical ecstasy, but they definitely go down well. Never very crowded, this is a cool place to kick back for awhile and drink a few Tsing-

Taos with your food, or, of course, the good Dr. Fong and one or two of his companions.

Seven Treasures

🍽 *2310 S. Wentworth Avenue 312-225-2668*
Hours: Sun–Thu, 11 A.M.–2 A.M.; Fri–Sat, 11 A.M.–2:30 A.M.

Large and brightly lit, this place can be a hazard to your eyes if you've just come from a dim bar, but late at night no one seems to mind—this place gets hopping. The menu is large and the portions huge, but your best bet is a noodle dish. Not only is this their speciality, but a big old bowlful is extremely cheap.

Joy Yee

🍽 *2159 S. China Place 312-328-0001*
Hours: Open every day, 11 A.M.–10:30 P.M.

This little pan-Asian noodle shop is always hopping, serving up some very tasty dishes, in particular the Vietnamese noodles with beef. You can also get plenty of Chinese and Thai standards, as well as a huge assortment of drinks, from bubble teas to fruit juices and freezes. Joy Yee is a little more expensive than surrounding eateries, but the atmosphere is much more upbeat.

Ken–Kee Restaurant

🍽 *2129-A S. China Place 312-326-2088*
Hours: Open every day, 11 A.M.–1 A.M.

Ken-Kee in Chinatown Square is an interesting place. Here you can get everything from congee and rice dishes to bubble teas and spaghetti, not to mention condensed milk toast. According to my wife, who spent most of her teen years in Hong Kong, this is exactly the type of eatery you find everywhere in Hong Kong. This is borne out by the large numbers of Chinatown residents who eat here—and at the Chinatown Square establishments in general as opposed to those on Wentworth Avenue, which are geared more for the tourists. I've always been fine with whatever I've ordered here, but my wife gets particularly excited over what she refers to as the congee with ghost bones. No, "ghost bones" is not a euphemism for something bizarre like chicken feet (which my wife claims are very tasty), but simply for deep-fried dough fritters. Whatever the case, Ken-Kee is cheap and well worth a visit.

Aji Ichiban

2117 S. China Place 312-328-9998
Hours: Mon–Thu, 11 A.M.–8 P.M.; Fri, 11 A.M.–9 P.M.;
Sat, 10 A.M.–9 P.M.; Sun, 10 A.M.–8 P.M.

My wife goes ga-ga over this place. In this small shop you'll find all sorts of Japanese and Chinese candies— the classics, according to the woman. Now though I've begun to lose my taste for sugary candy (as one gets older one's teeth gain in importance), I can certainly see the value in such a place. My wife, however, always stocks up on the sour candies and dried plums, so I'm afraid I've yet to develop any appreciation for the Japanese and Chinese "classics." All you young'uns with your pearly white chompers will have to mosey on in and sample the wares yourself.

Hit Music

2105 S. China Place 312-326-3222
Hours: Open every day, 10:30 A.M.–7 P.M.

This shop is very convenient, for within its confines you can stock up on your favorite Asia-pop CDs, karoake VCDs, and oven range hoods. *Ai ya!*

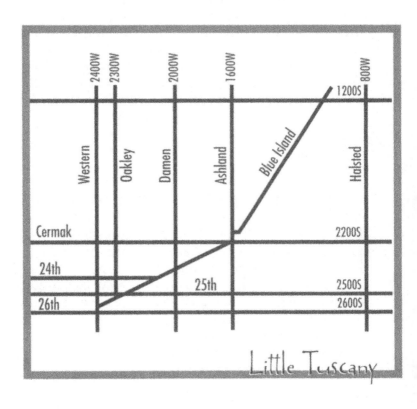

32

LITTLE TUSCANY

This is a very small area in Pilsen. Back before the 1920s, a large settlement of northern Italians from the Tuscany region settled here to work in the McCormick Reaper factory. Only a few blocks remain, but it is surprising admist all the Mexican residents to suddenly come upon a handful of Italian restaurants. Prices aren't cheap here, but if you're looking for some good Italian food, this is definitely a place to visit.

Ignotz Ristorante

2421 S. Oakley Avenue 773-579-0300
*Hours: Tue–Thu, 11 A.M.–10 P.M.; Fri, 11 A.M.–
11 P.M.; Sat, 4 P.M.–11 P.M.; Sun, 3 P.M.–9 P.M.*

This attractive, casual little place serves up a good selection of entrées, with their stuffed gnocchi and veal parmesan registering high on my list of favorites. Ignotz is a bit of an exception to the high prices you'll find at most of the restaurants here. While certainly not cheap, it is very reasonable, and the atmosphere and staff are first rate.

Bruna's Ristorante

2424 S. Oakley Avenue 773-254-5550
Hours: Mon–Thu, 11 A.M.–10 P.M.; Fri–Sat, 11 A.M.–11 P.M.;
Sun, 1 P.M.–10 P.M.

Serving up Northern Italian cuisine, Bruna's is definitely expensive, with pasta bowls going for at least eleven dollars and entrées above fifteen dollars. I must say, however, that if you don't mind spending some money, this is an intimate, comfortable restaurant, with classy, dim lighting and outstanding food. But remember, when I said pasta bowls, I meant bowls. The portions are huge. Don't expect to hop from here to some dance club; you'll be holding your belly with a dazed grin instead.

Miceli's Deli & Foodmart

2448 S. Oakley Avenue 773-847-6873
Hours: Mon–Fri, 8 A.M.–6:30 P.M.; Sat, 8 A.M.–4 P.M.

This deli is a great place to get a sandwich or pick up various foodstuffs such as pasta, cheeses, and meats. They also have a great selection of Italian spices.

33

BRIDGEPORT

B ridgeport has been around for a long time—almost for as long as Chicago has officially been a city. Irish immigrants flocked here to work on the Illinois-Michigan Canal, establishing a shanty town in what soon became known as Bridgeport. Though the Irish weren't received very well by the U.S.-born Yankees—one *Chicago Tribune* editorial declared they had smaller brains than the average Anglo-Saxon—they soon came to dominate the police force and the political system of Chicago. Bridgeport is still a hard-nosed, working-class neighborhood, and from this base Richard J. Daley began his dynasty as Chicago mayor from 1955 until his death in 1976. His son, Richard M., now has the reigns, and though his machine may be a bit more subtle, it is no less effective at keeping him and his people in office.

Bridgeport has made national news a few times due to racial incidents. Most notably, it was here that the Rev. Martin Luther King, Jr. got pelted with a brick while leading a march through the neighborhood. More recently, Bridgeport was the scene of a nasty beating. Leonard Clark—a thirteen-year-old African American boy—was beaten into a coma and

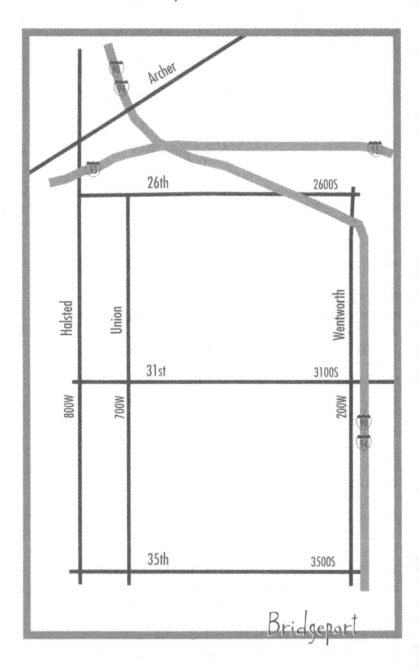

brain-damaged by a group of eighteen-to-twenty-year-old white youths. The trial of one of these kids was delayed a number of times. Of the two witnesses, one was murdered in an "unrelated" robbery attempt, while the other disappeared in Arizona, only to resurface after the trial. Could it be coincidence that the father of the latter youth has mob ties? Or that the one kid who did go on trial also has a father connected to the mob?

But hell, Bridgeport isn't all that bad. The legendary racial animosity Bridgeport's whites are known for is pretty much a thing of the past, except in certain pockets. Plenty of Mexicans live here, and the eastern portion of Bridgeport, where my wife and I live, is almost entirely Chinese. In fact, Chinese realty and construction companies are very active here, erecting condo developments wherever possible, just like in Chinatown. However, those aforementioned white "pockets" remain, and their residents are very clannish, most of them having lived their entire lives within a few blocks of the home they were born in. Therefore I'd advise against going into most of the bars in this neighborhood without a local "sponsor," as it's more likely than not that you will be made to feel like an unwelcome outsider. When all talk ceases the moment you open the door, it's usually a good sign to turn right around and leave. Follow this advice and all will be well.

Benedict's Delicatezzi Italiano

¶◯¶ 2501 S. Archer Avenue 312-225-1122
Hours: Mon–Fri, 6 A.M.–3 P.M.; Sat, 8 P.M.–2 P.M.

This little corner deli makes the best subs in Bridgeport. Most of the subs are heavy on Italian meats and cheeses, though they do make a regular old "Chicago sub" with roast beef and American or Swiss cheese. The Italian subs, however, are the main attraction. Along with the subs you can get your typical burgers and dogs and Italian sausage, though they also make a variety of salads, both leafy and otherwise. The pesto and pasta salad, in particular, is very good.

Sugar Shack

¶○¶ 630 W. Twenty-sixth Street 312-949-1153
Hours: Mon–Sat, 5 P.M.–11 P.M., May through October

This little ice cream stand is a handy place to hit. You order from the sidewalk, fork over your money, and before you know it you're on your way with a very tasty malt or banana split or ice cream cone or even—if you're of a peculiar frame of mind—a hot dog. On summer nights this is a neighborhood favorite.

Ricobene's

¶○¶ 252 W. Twenty-sixth Street 312-225-5555
Hours: Mon–Thu, 11 A.M.–12:30 A.M., Fri–Sat, 11 A.M.–2 A.M., Sun, 11:30 A.M.–12 A.M.

One of the South Side's finest fast-food joints, Ricobene's serves up your typical burgers and pizza along with pasta and a variety of specialty sandwiches. The main attraction, however, is their Italian breaded steak sandwich. To the best of my knowledge, this sandwich is a purely (South Side) Chicago invention, and Ricobene's does it up the best. What is an Italian breaded steak sandwich? Heaps of flank steak coated in breading, fried, then dumped on an Italian roll and covered in red sauce. Hot peppers and shredded mozzarella cheese are then slathered over it. It's one of the best damn sandwiches you'll ever have. And fully loaded it'll set you back only four bucks. For non–meat eaters, they make a tasty breaded eggplant sandwich. The fresh-cut fries are excellent as well.

Maxwell Street Depot

¶○¶ 411 W. Thirty-first Street 312-326-3514
Hours: Open 24 hours

Ever had a pork chop sandwich? Well, this is the place to get one. Slathered in fried onions, you'll find this puppy goes down well in the wee hours after a bender. It doesn't necessarily come out the other end as pleasantly the next day, but hell, every now and then it's worth it.

Unique Thrift Store

3000 S. Halsted Street 312-842-0942
Hours: Mon–Sat, 8 A.M.–9 P.M.; Sun, 10 A.M.–5 P.M.

Unlike most of the Unique "chain," this one is bright, somewhat airy, and relatively untrampled. It's definitely worth your time to take a look here.

Pancho Pistolas

700 W. Thirty-first Street 312-225-8808
*Hours: Mon–Thu, 11 A.M.–11 P.M.; Fri–Sat, 11 A.M.–
12 A.M.; Sun, 11 A.M.–10 P.M.*

If this place was located in one of the hipper neighborhoods up north I probably wouldn't even mention it, since such places are not hard to find in such locations. In Bridgeport, however, Pancho Pistolas is an anomaly. A rather "upscale" Mexican restaurant—there's even outdoor seating in the summer—Pancho's serves up your typical burritos and tacos as well as chimichangas, enchiladas, and various fancy meat entrées. The prices are a bit steep compared to a typical taqueria, but for the high-quality fare you get here, they're well worth it. A convivial, fun place to eat.

Game Kingdom

610 W. Thirty-first Street 312-225-5740
*Hours: Mon–Fri, 12 P.M.–9 P.M.; Sat, 12 P.M.–8 P.M.;
Sun, 12 P.M.–6 P.M.*

Here in this little shop you'll find plenty of new comics, fantasy role-playing card games, and various figurines and T-shirts. No, no Dungeons and Dragons stuff, folks. For those of us old enough to have whiled away our early teen years tucked away in the basement fighting imaginary orcs and dragons instead of hanging out with girls, we just have to accept the fact that the game has all but disappeared. This is most likely for the best. Start getting some of us geeks back into that game—especially those of us whose girl-meeting days are over—and we'd never have any reason to leave the basement.

Healthy Food Lithuanian Restaurant

3236 S. Halsted Street 312-326-2724
Hours: Mon–Sat, 7 A.M.–8 P.M.; Sun, 7 A.M.–5 P.M.

A throwback to the days when Bridgeport was home to a number of Lithuanian immigrants around the turn of the century, Healthy Food is one of the most erroneously named restaurants I've ever frequented. Healthy food indeed—if you're a peasant plowman. As for the rest of us, this is the type of fare that will clog your arteries and send your butt to the couch for a nap as soon as you get home. Along with standard American diner fare, you can also stuff down a number of traditional Lithuanian dishes such as blynai, which are pancakes served in a sort of "over easy" manner with your choice of fruit or cheese filling. The meat dumplings are good, but my favorite is the kugelis—a huge serving of potato pudding. Don't be intimidated by the waitress if she scoffs at you like a ninny if this is all you order. You probably won't even be able to finish it. The portions are gut-busting and the prices are cheap. As well, there are plenty of Lithuanian-themed paintings and carvings on the walls and various "objets d'art" for sale, including amber jewelry complete with trapped insects.

Let's Boogie Records and Tapes

3321 S. Halsted Street 312-254-0139
Hours: Tue–Sat, 12 P.M.–6 P.M.

A used record shop heavy on rock and R & B, Let's Boogie hasn't changed much over the years. You'll find plenty of vinyl, a boatload of cassettes, and a small selection of CDs. One major drawback with the CDs is that they're kept behind the counter or in display cases, so you can't browse through the titles as conveniently as you would like. What's interesting is some of the CDs you can find here—oddities you wouldn't expect to see in such a place, such as a Sisters of Mercy compilation and a recording (bootleg? I didn't say bootleg) of the Replacements' 1991 Grant Park concert, which—correct me if I'm wrong—was one of their last performances. Or was it their last Chicago performance? Whatever the case, Let's Boogie isn't necessarily worth a trip to the neighborhood itself, but if you're going to be here anyway, you should definitely stop in.

Puffer's

3356 S. Halsted Street 773-927-6073
Hours: Open every day, 2 P.M.–2 A.M.

Much like Pancho Pistolas is the only northside-esque restaurant in Bridgeport, this small tavern is the only northside-esque bar; it's also the only bar in the neighborhood where you won't get the hairy eyeball upon entering. Though Puffer's clientele is made up mostly of native Bridgeportians, the atmosphere here is very laid-back, friendly, and, surprisingly enough, somewhat bohemian. The owner loves music and you can sometimes catch a jam session in back. There are also plenty of good beers on tap—this may be the only Bridgeport bar where you don't have to drink Old Style.

Comiskey Park (or, if I must, "U. S. Cellular Field")

333 W. Thirty-fifth Street 312-674-1000
Hours: Varies; check paper or call ahead for game times

Sure, the new stadium is very mall-like, the concession food is the same quality as convenience-store trash, and the beer (outside of what they serve at the bar in center field) is exclusively Miller Genuine Goat Piss or Lite, but hey, on Tuesdays through Thursdays you can get in for cheap. This is supposed to relegate you to the Everest-like upper deck, but why bother when there are plenty of available seats in other parts of the stadium? I mean let's face it, even when the Sox are doing well, this place rarely seems to get packed. Just don't wear any Cub paraphernalia. This is the South Side, ya mook, where dey don't like dem Cubbies.

34

LITTLE VILLAGE

Nestled in the shadow of Cook County Jail, Little Village is a slightly more upscale version of Pilsen. It is to Little Village or the suburbs that many of Pilsen's residents finally move after saving up money for a house. Just like in Pilsen, Mexicans began replacing the original white ethnics in the 1950s. Many were stuck here until fairly recently as the suburbs to the west— namely Cicero—were notoriously racist. Though that situation has certainly changed, many homeowners have remained anyway. Here you'll find a long strip of restaurants, groceries, and shops catering primarily to the local clientele.

Puerto Mexico #2

3235 W. Twenty-sixth Street 773-247-4651
Hours: Open every day, 8 A.M.–2 A.M.

This taqueria is a great place for take-out, though you can certainly kick back at a table if you so desire. Prices are cheap and the food is better than at many similar such joints. The tacos are particularly good—and tacos are not usually something I find myself recommending.

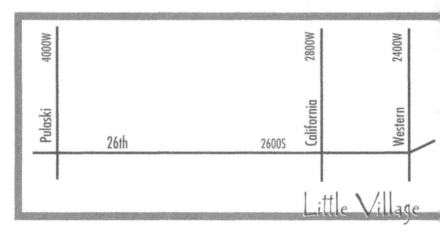

Village Discount Outlet

4020 W. Twenty-sixth Street
Hours: Mon–Fri, 9 A.M.–9 P.M.; Sat, 9 A.M.–6 P.M.;
Sun, 11 A.M.–5 P.M.

Yes, they are everywhere. This one is bigger than most and slightly less picked over considering its out-of-the-way location. Still, I make no guarantees.

Big Mega Music Strip

3100 block to 3300 block of W. Twenty-sixth Street

No, thank the heavens, there is no particular store with the above name. But over a two-block stretch of Twenty-sixth Street you'll find more record stores than you can shake a stick at. If you're into Latin music, you should definitely hit this strip, as the various shops cater to a whole slew of styles.

35

HYDE PARK

Hyde Park is known for the University of Chicago, one the country's most prestigious schools. Founded in 1892 near the lake in what was then a wealthy, primarily Jewish neighborhood, the university has continued to reside amid very desirable real estate. But know that this desirable real estate comprises only a few square blocks. Surrounding it is cheap, dilapidated housing occupied entirely by African Americans. There are, of course, plenty of affluent and middle-class African Americans living among the whites in Hyde Park, but the contrast to the adjoining neighborhoods is impossible to miss. After the fall of the Berlin Wall, the *Chicago Reader* joked that Hyde Park had put in a bid to buy it for themselves.

Whatever the case, Hyde Park is definitely something to see, from its old houses and three-flats to the stately university buildings themselves. Just walking down the block makes you feel scholarly and Victorian. And it was here in Jackson Park by the lake that the World's Columbian Exposition took place in 1893. The building housing the Museum of Science and Industry was built for the fair, as well as a mock "White City" and the world's first Ferris Wheel.

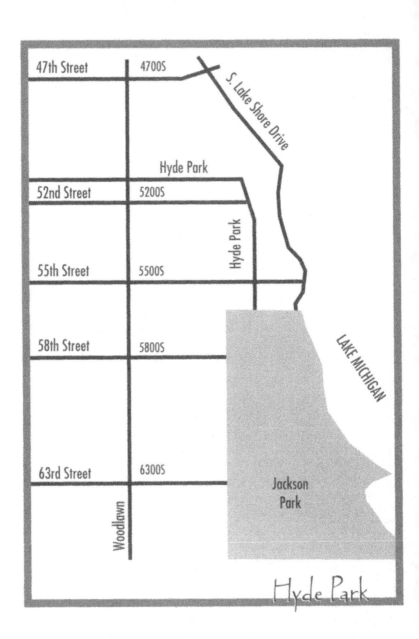

Visitors to the event marveled at all the high-tech gadgets and innovations on display, much in the same way that we're impressed at electronic trade shows. So hey, even if you don't care about all the great bookstores in the neighborhood, at least come for the history.

Dixie Kitchen

5225 S. Harper Avenue #A 773-363-4943
Hours: Sun–Thu, 11 A.M.–10 P.M.; Fri–Sat, 11 A.M.–11 P.M.

If you like southern and New Orleans–style cooking, you can't leave the city without hitting this place. This hopping, convivial place serves up some of the best grub north of the Mason-Dixon Line. Crawfish étouffées, chicken fried steak, gumbo, fried oysters, corn fritters, black-eyed peas, red beans and rice—you name it, they serve it. The food is outstanding, the portions huge, and the prices fairly cheap. And to accompany your meal, what else but Dixieland and zydeco tunes. A great place.

Dr. Wax

5225 S. Harper Avenue #D 773-493-8696
Hours: Mon–Sat, 11 A.M.–8 P.M.; Sun, 12 P.M.–6 P.M.

Unlike its comfortably frumpy cousin up north, this is a sleek, upscale Dr. Wax. Though they do boast a small selection of vinyl, the primary stock is CDs. And rock is the secondary category here. R&B and jazz is the style du jour, only here you'll find mostly current artists. If this is your cup of tea, this is one of the better record shops in town.

Scholar's Bookstore

1379 E. Fifty-third Street 773-288-6565
Hours: Mon–Thu, 10 A.M.–6 P.M.; Fri–Sat, 10 A.M.–7 P.M.

 This spartan, no-frills shop specializes in Chinese-language books as well as English-language books about China and Asia. They also sport a small fiction and martial arts section. In addition to books, they sell a large collection of Chinese videos as well as a number of used computer programs.

2nd Hand Tunes

1377 E. Fifty-third Street 773-684-3375
Hours: Open every day, 10 A.M.–8 P.M.

This Hyde Park location stocks much more vinyl than CDs, and specializes in R&B and jazz rather than rock like the Clark Street store up north. Still, you can find plenty of rock at the usual decent prices. If you prefer R&B and jazz, however, you'll be quite pleased; their collection is very thorough.

Jimmy's Woodlawn Tap

1172 E. Fifty-fifth Street 773-643-5516
Hours: Mon–Fri, 10:30 A.M.–2 A.M.; Sat, 10:30 A.M.–3 A.M.;
Sun, 11 A.M.–2 A.M.

The Woodlawn Tap has been serving up the suds for over fifty years, and I wouldn't be surprised if in all that time the interior hasn't changed one bit. A very no-frills, well-worn shack of a joint, you'll find simple beers on tap, simple sandwiches served up from the simple kitchen, and plenty of simple chairs and tables throughout the bar. The prices are pretty simple too. And this place doesn't just cater to the college folk, but quite an assortment of old-timers as well. Then again, maybe the latter were college folk some fifty years back and just can't bring themselves to leave. Whatever the case, this is a great, low-key place in which to down a few.

Ex Libris Theological Books

1340 E. Fifty-fifth Street 773-955-3456
Hours: Mon–Sat, 12 P.M.–6 P.M.

This used bookstore has an outstanding collection, with books ranging in topics from scholarly biblical studies to Buddhism, church histories, and sociological studies of various religions. The prices are very expensive, but then most of the volumes are from university presses. You're paying for their rarity as well. I mean let's face it, the average consumer isn't looking for a lengthy tome exploring the impact the concept of Satan has had on Western culture, is he? Outside of a library, Ex Libris is pretty much the only place you're going to be lucky enough to find most of these titles.

Powell's Bookstore

1501 E. Fifty-seventh Street 773-955-7780
Hours: Open every day, 9 A.M.–11 P.M.

As is usually the case, this Powell's is a great place to spend hours browsing. Prices are cheaper here than in most used stores, and they even have a bargain basement with a smattering of fairly good titles. Their literature collection is first rate, as are the Native American and history section. They also stock plenty of art and photography books. And if literary criticism is your thing (God help you), you'll be fit to be tied. Their collection of titles is enormous.

O'Gara & Wilson Ltd.

1448 E. Fifty-seventh Street 773-363-0993
Hours: Mon–Sat, 9 A.M.–10 P.M.; Sun, 12 P.M.–10 P.M.

This immaculate, "old school" bookshop contains a good general selection of books, all of them in tip-top shape. Prices are a bit up there, but they have some great titles, especially when it comes to history. The section on the middle ages is particularly thorough. You can learn about everything from the Crusades to Charlemagne's sex life. They say he was a man of great stature.

57th Street Books

1301 E. Fifty-seventh Street 773-684-1300
Hours: Mon–Thu, 10 A.M.–10 P.M.; Fri–Sat, 10 A.M.–11 P.M.;
Sun, 10 A.M.–8 P.M.

This is one of the best stores selling new books in
Chicago. In five brick, den-like rooms, you'll find a
great collection of books. Everything from politics to
children's picture books, literature to sci-fi is offered
here, as well as quality periodicals. You may not find
the latest self-help books or Tom Clancy novel, but
good, thoughtful works from a large collection of pub-
lishers—both mainstream and independent. Various
readings and workshops also take place here.

Seminary Co-op Bookstore

5757 S. University Avenue 773-752-4381
Hours: Mon–Fri, 8:30 A.M.–9 P.M.; Sat, 10 A.M.–6 P.M.;
Sun, 12 P.M.–6 P.M.

Located in the basement of the beautiful old Chicago
Theological Seminary, this nationally known bookstore
is a sprawling warren full of outstanding works. In fact,
the Seminary Co-op deserves the title of Chicago's best
bookstore, featuring thousands of new books with a
heavy emphasis on scholarly works in the fields of
sociology, history, and the humanities. You can literally
spend hours here scanning all the different titles and
still only scratch the surface of their inventory. No trip
to Chicago is complete without at least one visit here.
Expect to leave sweaty and content.

Information

If you're looking to see what particular bands are playing on any given night or what bar specials are being offered about town, there are a number of free publications in Chicago that will tell you just that. There are also a few online sources as well. Here are the best of them:

The Chicago Reader

Hands down the best free weekly publication in these here United States. Within the Reader's four thick and meaty sections you'll find great feature stories and articles, reviews, classifieds, and a comprehensive listing of what band, art shows, movies, and plays are in town for the week. The Reader comes out on Thursdays and can be picked up just about anywhere on the North Side, from book and record stores to supermarkets.

The Onion

Chicago is one of the lucky cities to be treated to a free weekly print version of The Onion. This parody newspaper, which originates in Madison, Wisconsin, is not be missed. It's one of the funniest papers you'll come across. While the second half of the paper is devoted to interviews and event listings, it's the first half you'll really want to see. If you haven't discovered The Onion yet in its print, online, or book form, trust me: you need to check it out. It comes out every Thursday and can be found in many North Side record and book stores, as well as a variety of vintage shops.

www.metromix.com

This Web site is the best of those devoted to Chicago happenings. It gives you information on everything from the weather and traffic patterns to what's going on in various restaurants and nightclubs. It also features plenty of articles on a variety of topics and you can also listen to demo tapes by local bands.

Two other Web sites that offer local information are www.centerstage.net and www.4chicago.com.

General Index

Category Index

About the Author

Bill Franz was born in suburban Chicago and has lived in the city for fifteen years. A graduate of Columbia College, he has worked a variety of jobs as he has pursued a writing career.

9 781681 629254